"Dr Sandeep Goel has an extraordinary ability to demystify the intimidating world of finance, making it accessible and understandable for everyone. He transforms the complex concepts into easily digestible chunks of wisdom that makes even the most novice reader feel confident. I am sure that Dr Goel has truly created a resource that would empower beginners to navigate the financial landscape with ease and understanding."

—**Mr. Deepak Sharma**, *Advisor, Telecom Regulatory Authority of India, GoI, New Delhi*

"Being financially informed is an indispensable life skill. This book structures and presents financial concepts clearly and concisely and explains their applications in managing finances. It is an invaluable resource for finance professionals as well as amateurs, and even those fearful of finance."

—**Dr. Niti Nandini Chatnani**, *Professor of Finance, Indian Institute of Foreign Trade, New Delhi*

Finance for Beginners

This book takes readers through the world of finance from a lay-person's perspective. It presents, clarifies and illustrates the fundamental concepts of financial proficiency to all who don't have prior knowledge or expertise in financial matters. The author further outlines the financial operations of business firms and individuals in a clear and accessible manner.

The book:

- Discusses the fundamentals of finance and accounting.
- Provides an understanding of financial statements for managerial decision-making.
- Includes financial analysis for resource allocation and shareholders' wealth maximisation.
- Discusses management of finances and investments in day-to-day lives.

Presenting current global trends and real-world cases in finance and richly illustrated with tables and figures, this volume will be indispensable for individuals, business managers and management students pursuing courses related to financial accounting. It will also be an important resource for executive and management development programmes (EDPs and MDPs) as well as professionals interested in a short refresher course on finance.

Sandeep Goel is Senior Professor of Accounting and Finance and Corporate Governance at Management Development Institute (MDI) Gurgaon, India. He holds two doctorates, one in finance;

and another in accounting from the Faculty of Management Studies, University of Delhi. He completed his bachelor's with honours and master's degrees in commerce with specialisation in finance from Shri Ram College of Commerce and the Department of Commerce, Delhi School of Economics, University of Delhi, respectively. He has three decades of industry and academic experience across various organisations and institutions of repute, including the Shri Ram Group, the University of Delhi and MDI Gurgaon. He sits as an independent director on the Board of Machino Plastics Ltd., Gurugram, a Suzuki JV. He is Visiting Professor of the Faculty of Management, University of Lodz, Poland, and Aix-Marseille Graduate School of Management – IAE AIX-Marseille University, France. He is a management trainer and consultant to organisations like Maruti Suzuki, Canara Bank, JK Tyre, PFRDA, NPCI, IRS, ITS, FIA Business School (Brazil), Bata, Encore, Federal-Mogul Goetze (India) Ltd., SOS Village International, Cairns India, National Banking Institute (Nepal), Druk Holdings (Bhutan), UltraTech Cements, ONGC and many more. He is a prolific writer and has authored more than 15 books and published over 100 research articles and cases in national and international journals of repute. He has been conferred with the Award for Excellence in Teaching, 2023–24, 2015–16, and the Award for Excellence in Research, 2015–16, at MDI.

Foundations of Finance

Series author: Sandeep Goel

is a Senior Professor of Accounting and Finance, and Corporate Governance, Management Development Institute (MDI) Gurgaon, India.

This series presents the foundations of financial knowledge in a lucid and accessible format. The books in the series deal with critical themes in financial literacy and proficiency today, such as financial accounting, cost accounting, corporate finance, contemporary finance, forensic accounting, fraud analytics, and fraud risk management. Each volume in the series deals with updated expert insights, current global trends, and real-world cases in finance and is richly illustrated with tables, figures, and learning tools. The individual books in the series will be indispensable for individuals, business managers, and management students pursuing undergraduate and postgraduate courses in finance. They will also be important resources for executive and management development programmes (EDPs & MDPs) as well as beginners and professionals interested in a short refresher course on finance and financial management.

Finance for Beginners
Sandeep Goel

Finance for Beginners

Sandeep Goel

Routledge
Taylor & Francis Group
LONDON AND NEW YORK

Designed cover image: Getty Images

First published 2026
by Routledge
4 Park Square, Milton Park, Abingdon, Oxon OX14 4RN

and by Routledge
605 Third Avenue, New York, NY 10158

Routledge is an imprint of the Taylor & Francis Group, an informa business

British Library Cataloguing-in-Publication Data
A catalogue record for this book is available from the British Library

ISBN: 978-1-041-21223-2 (hbk)
ISBN: 978-1-041-22008-4 (pbk)
ISBN: 978-1-003-73014-9 (ebk)

DOI: 10.4324/9781003730149

Typeset in Sabon
by Apex CoVantage, LLC

Contents

Figures

Tables

Preface

Managing your personal finance is the dream run for every individual. Likewise, knowing your organisation's financial health is the central aspect of managerial decision-making and control. An effective manager is one who is able to (i) analyse financial performance trends, (ii) make timely decisions and (iii) modify planned and future activities to mitigate various risks. This is where 'financial proficiency and efficiency' assumes importance at all levels of business and in all types of organisations internationally.

Objective

This book will help not only to develop an understanding of the concepts of accounting and finance at a personal level but also to aid the managers to use it as an effective tool for financial analysis and managerial decision-making. It facilitates:

- What are the accounting nuances at the basic level?
- What financial statements are prepared and analysed as a part of financial reporting?
- How can financial statements be used for investment decision-making?
- How should the firm be managed to increase the wealth of shareholders?

It is for everyone who wants to learn finance. This book is equally useful to people with a finance background for advanced learning.

Features

The book contains a number of learning aids like figures, tables, illustrations and case studies on finance acumen to facilitate learning. Real-world cases of corporate organisations have been analysed and discussed from diverse sectors for gaining financial insights and perspectives. These companies have international operations, so they will be of immense use to readers worldwide. All these features will make the book more interesting and relevant to readers.

Organisation of the book

The book has been simply divided into four key chapters. It has been logically sequenced to facilitate better learning among the readers. Most chapters are self-contained and can be read independently of the others.

Chapter 1 'What is business?' provides an overview of different forms of business organisations operating in different parts of the world, including India.

Chapter 2 'The journey of accounting' explains accounting fundamentals and its process.

Chapter 3 'Understanding of financial statements' provides a platform for financial health from a common man's perspective.

Chapter 4 'Financial analysis for decision-making' examines the corporate financial statements with the help of various accounting tools like ratio analysis for knowing the financial performance of a business in detail.

This book will build up your finance excellence, which is important for your personal and professional success. This is a perfect blend of theory with practice. An attempt has been made to keep the book simple in nature yet comprehensive in approach. I am confident that the readers will find this book truly valuable in terms of its quality and presentation. Any constructive comments and suggestions for future improvement of the book are highly appreciated and welcome *at sandeepgoel1810@ gmail.com.*

Happy learning!

Acknowledgements

I wish to thank God Almighty for everything in life! The work would be incomplete if I did not acknowledge my parents' contribution. They have been a constant source of inspiration for me and have always stood by me through thick and thin. My wife provided her unstinted support and encouragement in completing the book. My daughter Maanya is my soul whose smile always keeps me going in life.

I am also thankful to the entire team of Routledge, New Delhi, including Dr. Shashank Sinha, Mr. Yogesh Srivastava and Ms. Anvitaa Bajaj, for their tremendous support and wholehearted cooperation at all stages of publication of this book.

My sincere thanks are also due to Mr. Deepak Sharma and Professor Niti Nandini Chatnani for their valuable support and endorsements to the book.

Last, but not least, I gratefully express my gratitude to the following fellow academic colleagues and professional associates for providing their invaluable advice and inputs for the enrichment of the book.

- **Dr. Brian P. Miller,** *Professor of Accounting, Warrington College of Business, University of Florida, USA*
- **Dr. Robert C. Rickards,** *Professor of Accounting, German Police University, Münster, Germany*
- **Dr. Maciej Turała,** *Vice Dean for International Relations, University of Lodz, Poland*
- **Mr. S. S. Sharma,** *IAS Retd., Former Secretary, Government of India, Gurugram*
- **Dr. J. P. Singh,** *Former Professor of Finance, Department of Management Studies, Indian Institute of Technology Roorkee*

- **Mr. Aditya Jindal,** *Chairman cum Managing Director, Machino Plastics Ltd., Gurugram*
- **Dr. Sonam Chawla,** *Associate Professor of Organizational Behaviour, O.P. Jindal Global University, Sonipat*
- **Dr. Vishakha Bansal,** *Assistant Professor of Finance & Control, Indian Institute of Management Shillong*
- **Dr. Ajay Kumar,** *Assistant Professor, Bharati Vidyapeeth Institute of Management & Research, New Delhi*

Abbreviations

ACP	Average collection period
AHP	Average holding period
AICPA	American Institute of Certified Public Accountants
A/P	Accounts payable
APP	Average payment period
A/R	Accounts receivable
ATR	Assets turnover ratio
BV	Book value per share
CAR	Capital adequacy ratio
CASA	Current and savings accounts ratio
CFF	Net cash flow from financing activities
CFI	Net cash flow from investing activities
CFO	Net cash flow from operating activities
CTR	Creditors turnover ratio
CWIP	Capital work in progress
D/E	Debt-equity ratio
D/P	Dividend pay-out ratio
DPS	Dividend per share
DSCR	Debt service coverage ratio
D/Y	Dividend yield ratio
DTR	Debtors turnover ratio
EBIT	Earnings before interest and tax
EBITDA	Earnings before interest, tax, depreciation and amortisation
EBT	Earnings before taxes
EPS	Earnings per share
GAAP	Generally accepted accounting principles
GCPL	Godrej Consumer Products Ltd.

GSFC	Gujarat State Fertilizers & Chemicals Ltd. (formerly Gujarat State Fertilizer Company Ltd.)
HUF	Hindu undivided family
HUL	Hindustan Unilever Ltd.
ICR	Interest coverage ratio
IFFCO	Indian Farmers Fertiliser Cooperative Limited
ITR	Inventory turnover ratio
JV	Joint venture
LIC	Life Insurance Corporation of India
LLP	Limited liability partnership
MNC	Multinational corporation
MSIL	Maruti Suzuki India Ltd.
MV	Market value
OPC	One-person company
PAT	Profit after taxes
P/B	Price to book ratio
PBDT	Profit before depreciation and tax
PBT	Profit before taxes
P/E	Price to earnings ratio
PSU	Public sector undertaking
ROCE	Return on capital employed
ROE	Return on equity
ROI	Return on investment
RONW	Return on net worth
SBI	State Bank of India
SLM	Straight-line method
TML	Tata Motors Ltd.
WCTR	Working capital turnover ratio
WDV	Written-down value

1 What is business?

The purpose of business organisations is to produce commodities or provide services to the community. Their activities are large-scale and have a significant impact on the society. The activities range from the provision of necessities to luxury and ultra-luxury, as well as services. Almost every aspect of a person's everyday life involves interaction with a business organisation. These business enterprises are unquestionably essential to the expansion of the economy and, in one way or another, affect every person.

Meaning of business organisation

A business organisation (also known as business enterprise, business undertaking, business firm or business concern) is an organisation that is engaged in some business or commercial activity. It may be owned and controlled by a single individual or by a group of individuals. So, a business organisation can be defined as 'an enterprise which produces, distributes or provides any product or service needed by the members of the community for a price'.

Types of business organisations

Business organisations may be classified into three broad categories as depicted in Figure 1.1.

DOI: 10.4324/9781003730149-1

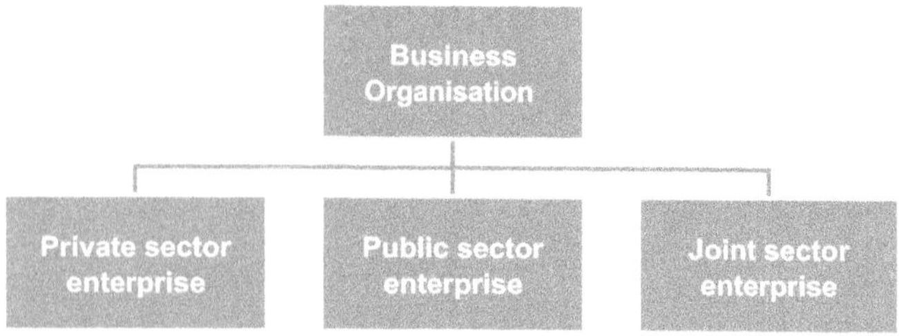

Figure 1.1 Classification of business organisations

Private sector enterprise

A private sector enterprise is owned, managed and controlled exclusively by private businessmen. There is no participation by the central or state governments in the establishment and ownership of a private enterprise. The main motive of a private enterprise is to earn profit (e.g., *Reliance Industries Ltd. (RIL), Infosys Ltd., Parle Products Pvt. Ltd., etc.*)

Public sector enterprise

A public sector enterprise is defined as an enterprise that may be (a) owned by the state, (b) managed by the state or (c) owned and managed by the state. According to Prof. A. H. Hanson, 'Public enterprise means state ownership and operation of industrial, agricultural, financial and commercial undertakings'.[1] The basic purpose of such undertakings is to render service to society (e.g., *Life Insurance Corporation of India (LIC), Steel Authority of India Limited (SAIL), Engineers India Ltd. (EIL), Delhi Transport Corporation (DTC))*.

Joint sector enterprise

Joint sector enterprises consist of those business undertakings wherein the ownership, management and control are shared jointly by the government, private entrepreneurs and the public. Joint sector enterprises have been designed as an effective instrument for exercising social control over industry (e.g., *Gujarat State*

Fertilizers & Chemicals Ltd. (GSFC) incorporated in 1962 as a joint sector enterprise set up by the Government of Gujarat. Its equity structure consisted of 49% of the state government and the rest of the public and financial institutions. Currently, the State Government has reduced its equity participation to 38.4%. The motive behind formation of this organisation was to support farmers).[2]

> Joint sector enterprise is not the same as 'Joint Venture' (JV), though in both the arrangements, two or more parties agree to pool their resources for the purpose of accomplishing a specific task. The basic difference between them is that 'a business relationship is needed for a joint venture but not for a joint enterprise'.

Types of private sector enterprises

Sole proprietorship

In this form of a business enterprise, a single person provides the entire capital, bears all the risks and manages the business. The proprietor is personally liable for all the debts of the firm. Thus, a sole proprietorship is a 'one-man army'. It is the simplest form of business to get started. *Small-scale businesses, like grocery stores and medical shops, operate as sole proprietorships.*

Joint Hindu family business

It may be defined as a form of business organisation in which all the male members of a Hindu undivided family carry on business under the management and control of the head of the family called 'Karta'. It is found only in India and is the result of the Hindu undivided family system followed in India.

Partnership

In this form of ownership, two or more persons enter into a contract to carry on some lawful activity jointly and to share its profits. Section 4 of the Indian Partnership Act, 1932, defines partnership as 'the relation between persons who have agreed to share the profits of a business carried on by all or any of them acting for all'.[3] Each partner is considered as the agent of the firm and of its partners. The firm has no separate legal entity from that of the partners. Each partner is jointly and individually liable for the debts of the firm to an unlimited extent.

> To form a partnership, as per the Companies Act 2013, there must be a minimum of 2 members to form a partnership, and the maximum number of members (partners) required should not be more than 100. **But, as per Rule 10 of Companies (Miscellaneous) Rules 2014, it should not exceed 50.**

Cooperative organisation

A cooperative society is a voluntary association of persons who join hands together to carry on economic activity of common need. It is based on the principles of mutual trust, equality, democracy and freedom. As an incorporated association of persons, it has a distinct entity and the liability of its members is limited. *IFFCO (Indian Farmers Fertiliser Cooperative Limited) is an example of a cooperative.*

Joint stock company

A joint stock company is an association of persons having a separate legal existence, perpetual succession and common seal. A company is an incorporated association of persons under the Companies Act, 2013, or the Companies Act, 1956. Its capital is generally divided into shares, which are transferable subject to certain conditions. Its management and control lie in the hands of the board of directors, consisting of the elected representatives of the members. A joint stock company in the private sector could be either a 'private ltd.' company or a 'public ltd.' company.

Private company

According to Section 2 (68) of the Companies Act, 2013, a private company has the following features:

i. The minimum paid-up share capital is Rs. 1 lakh.
ii. The company restricts the right to transfer its shares.
iii. The minimum number of members is two.
iv. The maximum number of members is 200.
v. It is prohibited from issuing shares to the public.

A private company must use 'Private Limited' as the last word (e.g., *Bikanervala Foods Pvt. Ltd*).

Public company

According to Section 2 (71) of the Companies Act, 2013, a public company has the following features:

i. It is not a private company.
ii. The minimum paid-up share capital is Rs. 5 lakh.
iii. The minimum number of members is seven.
iv. The maximum number of members is unlimited.
v. There is no restriction on the right of members to transfer their shares.
vi. The company is free to invite the general public to subscribe to its shares and debentures.

Such a company must use 'Limited' as the last word (e.g., Reliance Industries Ltd., Bajaj Auto Ltd.).

Table 1.1 lists the distinctions between private and public companies.

> As per **Companies (Amendment) Act, 2015**, the minimum paid-up share capital requirement of INR 100,000 (for a private company) and INR 500,000 (for a public company) under the Companies Act, 2013, has been removed.[4]

Table 1.1 Distinction between private and public companies

Nature	*Private Company*	*Public Company*
1. Meaning	Which by its article restricts: i. Numbers of members to 200 ii. Transfer of shares iii. Invitation of the public to subscribe its debenture, shares, etc. iv. Acceptance of deposits from the common public	Which is not private, and: i. No limit on maximum number of members ii. No restriction on the right of members to transfer their shares iii. Is free to invite the general public to subscribe to its shares and debentures
2. Law	Companies Act, 2013 and 1956	Companies Act, 2013 and 1956; SEBI Act, 1992; and allied laws
3. Minimum no. of shareholders (members)	2	7
4. Maximum no. of shareholders (members)	200	No limit
5. Minimum paid-up capital	Rs. 1,00,000	Rs. 5,00,000
6. Minimum no. of directors	2	3
7. Transferability of shares	Restricted	No restriction, if the company is listed on a stock exchange
8. Whole-time director (WTD)/ managing director (MD) appointment	Appointment not compulsory (Optional) and No restriction on appointment	Compulsory for (a) all listed companies (b) all specified public companies
9. Managerial remuneration	No restriction on the amount of managerial remuneration	Managerial remuneration is restricted and linked to Profits.

A holding company owns 20% or more shares of 'another company'. 'Another company' is further classified into:

(i) Subsidiary company = if 50% shares are owned by the holding company.
(ii) Associate company = if 20% or more shares are owned by the holding company.

One-person company

The Companies Act, 2013, introduces a new type of entity to the existing list of a public or private limited company, a 'one-person company' (OPC). An OPC means a company with only one person as its member, both minimum and maximum [Section 2 (62) of the Companies Act, 2013].

Section 3 classifies OPC as a private company for all legal purposes. All the provisions related to the private company are applicable to an OPC, unless otherwise expressly excluded.

The concept of OPC in the Indian legal system was introduced to encourage the corporatisation of micro businesses and entrepreneurship with a simpler legal regime. The most significant reason for shareholders to incorporate the 'single-person company' is 'the limited liability'. Though the concept of OPC is relatively

Limited liability partnership (LLP) is a corporate structure that combines the flexibility of a partnership of organising their internal management on the basis of a mutually arrived agreement and the advantages of limited liability of a company at a low compliance cost. Unlike the general partnerships in India, an LLP is a body corporate and legal entity separate from its partners and has perpetual succession, and any change in the partners of an LLP shall not affect the existence, rights or liabilities of the LLP. LLPs are governed by the provisions of the Limited Liability Partnership Act, 2008.

new in India, it has long been a very successful form of business in the UK and several Western countries.

Types of public sector enterprises

Public sector enterprises may be organised in any of the following types:

1 Departmental undertakings
2 Statutory corporations
3 Government companies

Departmental undertakings

Departmental undertaking is the oldest and traditional form of organising public sector enterprises. A departmental undertaking is managed by government officials under the supervision of the head of the department concerned. It may be run either by the central government or by a state government. The undertaking is under the overall and ultimate control of a minister who is responsible to parliament. *Examples are Indian Railways, Department of Post, Department of Telecommunication and defence establishments.*

Statutory corporations

A statutory corporation or a public corporation is a body set up under a special act of parliament or of the state legislature. It is known as a statutory corporation because it is created by a statute or law. The statute defines its objects, powers and functions. *Examples are Unit Trust of India (UTI), now UTI Asset Management Company Ltd., and Employees' State Insurance Corporation (ESIC).*

Government company

A government company or public sector undertaking (PSU) is a company in which not less than 51% of the paid-up share capital is held by the central government or by one or more state governments or jointly by the central and state governments. It is formed and registered under the Companies Act, 1956. *Examples are Steel Authority of India Limited (SAIL), Gas Authority of India Limited (GAIL) and Bharat Heavy Electricals Limited (BHEL).*

References

1 Hanson, Albert Henry. 1959. *Public Enterprise and Economic Development*. London: Routledge & Kegan Paul Ltd., p. 115.
2 NDTV Profit, Gujarat State Fertilizers & Chemicals Ltd. http://profit.ndtv.com/stock/gujarat-state-fertilizers-&-chemicals-ltd_gsfc/reports (accessed on 19 May 2017); https://www.ndtv.com/business/stock/gujarat-state-fertilizers-chemicals-ltd_gsfc/reports (accessed on 14 August 2023).
3 The Partnership Act, 1932 – Ministry of Corporate Affairs. www.mca.gov.in/Ministry/actsbills/pdf/Partnership_Act_1932.pdf, p. 3 (accessed on 1 July 2016).
4 Narsana, Bhavik, et al. 2015. *India: Companies (Amendment) Act, 2015: Key Highlights*. Khaitan & Co., July 6. http://www.mondaq.com/india/x/410320/Corporate+Commercial+Law/Companies+Amendment+Act+2015+Key+Highlights (accessed on 24 October 2016).

2 The journey of accounting

Accounting is coined as the 'language of business' because reports that are used by various interested parties are prepared and maintained, containing information on the activities and transactions of a business. This is the accounting purpose and application. It assists various firm stakeholders in making decisions by informing them of the outcomes of business operations. These stakeholders include the owner(s), investors, managers, creditors, regulators, government and other agencies.

Definition of accounting

The term 'accounting' refers to the processes carried out by the accountants of aggregating and shaping information into the financial reports that are meaningful to users of those reports. According to the American Institute of Certified Public Accountants (AICPA 1941), 'Accounting is the art of recording, classifying and summarising in significant manner and in terms of money, transactions and events which are, in part, at least of a financial character and interpreting the results thereof'.

> If accounting is looked at in a narrow perspective of *recording the business transactions only*, it is called 'bookkeeping'. So, bookkeeping is a part of accounting.

DOI: 10.4324/9781003730149-2

Every user draws on accounting information for various purposes, as follows:

- **Managers** need accounting information to make sound decisions about the day-to-day operations and growth of the business.
- **Owners (shareholders)** require it to find out the well-being of the business for protecting their hard-earned money invested in it.
- **Investors** use it for making profits.
- **Creditors** are always concerned about the entity's ability to repay its obligations.
- **Employees** need the information for evaluating the company's growth for their remuneration and incentives.
- **Government units** need information for tax and regulatory purposes.
- **Analysts** use accounting data to recommend investment strategies.

Branches of accounting

The diversity of interested parties and their diverse needs result in various forms of accounting, as depicted in Figure 2.1.

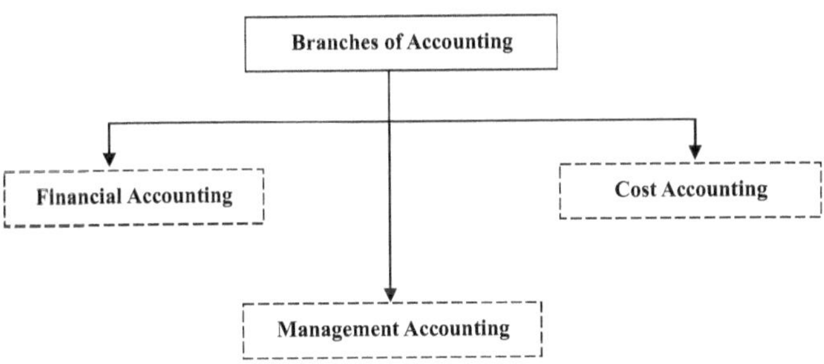

Figure 2.1 Accounting forms

Financial accounting

Financial accounting is the original form of accounting. It is mainly concerned with the financial performance of an organisation and involves the preparation of financial statements, the statement of profit and loss and the balance sheet for various stakeholders, like shareholders, debenture holders, creditors, banks and financial institutions. These financial reports are prepared under the relevant accounting principles and standards set by the respective standard-setting bodies. Financial accounting is external in nature.

Cost accounting

Cost accounting is the process of accounting for costs. 'It is the formal mechanism by means of which costs of products or services are ascertained and controlled'. It is a method of accounting in which all costs incurred in carrying out an activity are collected, classified and recorded. This data is then summarised and analysed to arrive at a selling price and/or to exercise cost control and determine where savings are possible.

Management accounting

It is the accounting for management, that is accounting which provides necessary information to the management for taking various decisions. Management accounting covers different areas of cost accounting, human resource accounting and so forth. Managerial accounting information is intended to serve the specific needs of management, like budgeting, product costing data, human performance and other details that are generally not reported on an external basis.

Objectives of accounting

The following are the main objectives of accounting:

1 **To keep systematic records.** Accounting is done to keep a systematic record of the financial transactions of an organisation. It makes the job of human beings easier.

2 **To ascertain profit or loss.** Accounting helps in ascertaining the net profit earned or loss suffered on account of business operations. This is done by keeping a proper record of revenues and expenses of a particular period in the form of a 'Statement of Profit and Loss'.
3 **To ascertain the financial position of the business.** This objective is served by the 'Balance Sheet' or 'Position Statement'. The balance sheet is a statement of assets and liabilities of the business on a particular date. It serves as a barometer for ascertaining the financial health of the business.
4 **To facilitate managerial decision-making.** Accounting records, analyses and reports information at various points of time to the required levels of authorities in order to facilitate decision-making.

Limitations of accounting

Accounting is not free from limitations either, explained as follows:

1 **Personal judgement.** A considerable amount of judgement and estimation is involved in maintaining and presenting the accounting information. *For example*, there is discretion involved in sales recognition, that is should sales be recorded on the dispatch of goods or the receipt of goods by the buyer? So, in order to present the information in a timely manner, various estimations are made in the preparation of financial reports.
2 **Historical nature.** Accounting is historical in nature. It presents information that has happened in the past. These records do not help in future planning and forecasting managerial implications.
3 **Cost principle.** Accounting information is recorded on a historical cost basis, instead of current or market value. *For example*, land is typically recorded and carried in the accounting records at the price at which it was purchased. This undermines the value of the business.
4 **No detailed information about the cost.** Financial accounting provides information as a whole in terms of income, expenses, assets and liabilities. It does not provide details of cost involved at the level of departments, processes, products, services or other units of activity within the organisation.

Accounting elements

The complete chart of the accounting elements is presented in Figure 2.2.

1. **Capital** – it is the money contributed by owners of the business. It denotes shareholders' funds in a business.
2. **Assets** – these are resources that are owned by a business, which have a monetary value, are used for generating return and can be converted into cash. They can be classified as:

    (i) ***Non-current assets/fixed assets*** – they are long-term resources, more than a year, and are used for long-term growth and expansion of a business, *like land and buildings, plant and machinery, furniture and fixtures and motor vehicles.*

Figure 2.2 Accounting elements

> Fixed assets can be further divided into 'tangible' and 'intangible' fixed assets.
>
> 'Tangible assets' include physical fixed assets, whereas 'intangible assets' include those that are not visible, such as goodwill, patents and copyrights.

(ii) ***Current assets*** – these are meant for current use and for day-to-day operations and are for less than a year, *like inventory, debtors (receivables), cash and bank.*

3. **Liability** – it is a debt or outstanding balance owed to another party, usually a supplier or lender, requiring a future cash flow for payment. It can be grouped as:

   (i) ***Non-current liability/long-term liability*** – these are for more than a year, *like term loans and debentures.*
   (ii) ***Current liability*** – these are for less than a year, *like creditors (payables) and bank overdraft.*

4. **Revenue** – it is the money that comes in on account of sales of goods or rendering of services. The term 'revenue' is used interchangeably with 'income'. It can be:

   (i) ***Operating revenue*** – it refers to the core income of the business, that is 'turnover' *or* 'sales and services'.
   (ii) ***Non-operating revenue*** – it is the income that comes from the non-core activities of the business, *like interest on investments and profit on the sale of fixed assets.*

5. **Expenses** – these are the costs that are incurred to run and maintain a business. These can be:

   (i) ***Operating expenses*** – these are the core expenses of business, *for example salaries, rent, printing and stationery, marketing expenses and so forth.*
   (ii) ***Non-operating expenses*** – these are related to the non-core activities of the business, *such as interest paid on loans.*

Example 2.1: Match the following items with their respective accounting categories of capital, asset, liability, revenue and expense.

S. No.	*Items*	*Categories*
1.	Machinery	Current Asset
2.	Shares Issued by SAIL	Non-current Liability
3.	Sales	Non-operating Income
4.	Borrowings from IFCI	Capital
5.	Cash and Bank Balance	Operating Expense
6.	Accounts Receivable	Non-current Asset
7.	Auditor's Fees	Current Asset
8.	Rent Payable	Operating Expense
9.	Power and Fuel	Current Liability
10.	Dividend Received	Operating Income

Solution

S. No.	*Items*	*Categories*
1.	Machinery	Non-current Asset
2.	Shares Issued by SAIL	Capital
3.	Sales	Operating Income
4.	Borrowings from IFCI	Non-current Liability
5.	Cash and Bank Balance	Current Asset
6.	Accounts Receivable	Current Asset
7.	Auditor's Fees	Operating Expense
8.	Rent Payable	Current Liability
9.	Power and Fuel	Operating Expense
10.	Dividend Received	Non-operating Income

Double-entry system of accounting

In accountancy, 'double entry accounting' is the basis or the standard system for businesses and other organisations to record financial transactions. The system is called 'double entry' because every transaction is considered to have two effects and is recorded in two accounts. Each transaction results in at least one account being debited and at least one account being credited, so that the total debits of the transactions equal the total credits.

The classification of debit and credit effects is structured in such a way that for each debit, there is a corresponding credit and vice versa. Hence, every transaction will have s 'dual' effect (i.e., debit effect and credit effect).

Debit and Credit

Under the 'double-entry system', two aspects of transactions are classified under the following types:

1 *Debit*
2 *Credit*

'Debit' is the portion of transaction that accounts for the increase in assets and expenses and the decrease in liabilities, equity and income. 'Credit' is the portion of a transaction that accounts for the increase in income, liabilities and equity and the decrease in assets and expenses.

***Example* 2.2**: Mr. James owns and operates a bookstore. He has identified the following transactions for the month of January 2024 that need to be accounted for in the monthly financial statements:

	Rs.
1. Payment of salary to staff	5,000
2. Sale of books for cash	10,000
3. Sale of books on credit	20,000
4. Purchase of furniture on credit from Smith	25,000
5. Interest paid on loans	1,000

Account for the above transactions under the double-entry system.

Solution

Under the double-entry system, the transactions will be accounted for as follows:

Account	*Effect*	*Debit*	*Credit*
		Rs.	Rs.
1. Salary expense	*Increase in expenses*	5,000	
Cash	*Decrease in assets*		5,000
2. Cash inflow	*Increase in assets*	10,000	
Sales	*Increase in income*		10,000
3. Accounts receivable	*Increase in assets*	20,000	
Sales	*Increase in income*		20,000
4. Furniture	*Increase in assets*	25,000	
Smith	*Increase in liabilities*		25,000
5. Interest paid	*Increase in expenses*	1,000	
Cash	*Decrease in assets*		1,000

In a **single-entry system**, only one aspect of a transaction is recognised. *For instance*, if a sale is made to a customer, only sales revenue will be recorded. However, the other side of the transaction relating to the receipt of cash or the grant of credit to the customer is not recognised.

The most common expression of double-entry system of accounting is the 'accounting equation', which is discussed as follows:

The accounting equation!

The accounting formula, also called the *balance sheet equation*, represents the relationship between the assets, liabilities and owner's equity of a business. It shows that the resources owned by a firm (its assets) are always equal to its obligations (its liabilities and capital). This relationship is expressed in the form of an equation:

$$\boxed{Assets = Liabilities + Owner's\ Capital}$$

This equation balances because everything the firm owns (assets) has to be purchased with something, either a liability or owner's capital. The terms of the accounting equation are defined below.

Assets

Assets, as mentioned above, are the economic resources of the entity and include items such as cash, stock, land, buildings and/or intangible assets like patents and copyrights. Assets are used to generate returns for the business.

Liabilities

Liabilities are the amounts owed to outsiders in the form of loans and credit. It is an 'existing' obligation to pay.

Owner's equity

Owner's equity is the owner's 'interest' in the business. In a sole proprietorship, the equity would typically consist of a single owner's capital account. Conversely, in a partnership, equity consists of separate capital accounts for each partner. Finally, in a corporate, the ownership interest is represented by shares (stock). The total owner's equity (i.e., 'stockholders' equity') of a corporate consists of shareholders' initial capital and reserves and surplus.

The following example explains the accounting equation mechanism.

Case let:

1 Anil and Bros. start a small business of hosiery goods with Rs. 10,000 of capital.

$$\boxed{\text{Assets} = \text{Liabilities} + \text{Capital}}$$

$$\text{Rs. } 10{,}000 = 0 + \text{Rs. } 10{,}000$$

Note: It increases cash as an asset and also increases the owner's equity.

2 Next, they spend Rs. 1,500 on office consumables. Now, the accounting equation looks like this:

$$\boxed{\text{Assets} = \text{Liabilities} + \text{Capital}}$$

$$\text{Rs. } 8,500 = 0 + \text{Rs. } 8,500$$

Note: It will reduce cash as an asset, and expenses decrease the owner's equity. So, in every case the accounting equation stays balanced.

Basis of accounting

Cash basis of accounting is the more popular method of recording and reporting small business income and expenses. In the cash accounting method, income and expenses are recorded only when funds are received or disbursed.

Accrual basis of accounting allows the income to be recorded when a sale is made, irrespective of the fact whether payment is received or not. Expenses are recorded when they are incurred, without being paid.

One of the accounting rules is that, with few exceptions, reports of the income of a business should be prepared on the *accrual basis*.

Then, what is the rationale of *cash basis accounting*? The answer is that the cash basis book-keeping is very simple, and for small firms, it may be adequate. Therefore, small-scale organisations, professionals like doctors and lawyers, follow cash basis accounting for their tax returns and other purposes.

Example 2.3: During 2023–24, A Ltd. had cash sales of Rs. 1,80,000 and credit sales of Rs. 3,60,000. Their expenses for the year were Rs. 2,40,000, out of which Rs. 80,000 is still to be paid. Commission received in the current year, due of last year, is Rs. 5,000. Interest due on investments for the year is Rs. 20,000.

Find out their profit/loss for 2023–24 as per:

1 Cash basis of accounting
2 Accrual basis of accounting

Solution

1. Profit/loss as per Cash basis:	
Revenue (cash inflow or cash sales)	Rs. 1,80,000
+ Commission received, due of last year	5,000
	1,85,000
Less: Expenses (cash outflow) (Rs. 2,40,000 – Rs. 80,000)	1,60,000
Profit	**Rs. 25,000**
2. Profit/loss as per Accrual basis:	
Revenue (total sales)	Rs. 5,40,000
+ Interest due on investments	20,000
	5,60,000
Less: Total expenses for the year	2,40,000
Profit	**Rs. 3,20,000**

Accounting process

Accounting process (cycle) refers to the specific tasks involved in completing an accounting process. The accounting process is expressed through the following stages (functions) of accounting:

1 **Recording.** This is the basic function of accounting. It is essentially concerned with ensuring that all business transactions of financial character are recorded in an orderly manner. Recording is done in the primary book, called a 'Journal'.

   The journal book may be further subdivided into various subsidiary books, such as cash journal (for recording cash transactions), purchases journal (for recording credit purchases of goods) and sales journal (for recording credit sales of goods). The number of subsidiary books to be maintained varies according to the nature and size of the business.

2 **Classifying.** Classification is concerned with categorising the recorded data and grouping the transactions or entries of a similar nature into one place. The work of classification is done in the book termed as 'Ledger'.

   The ledger book contains on different pages individual account heads under which all financial transactions of a similar nature are placed. *For example*, there may be separate account heads for sales, purchases, office expenses and so on. This will help in finding out the total balance under each of those heads.

3 **Summarising.** This involves the presentation of the classified data in a manner that is understandable and useful to the end users of accounting information. This process leads to the preparation of the following statements: *(i) Trial Balance, (ii) Income Statement and (iii) Balance Sheet*

4 **Analysing and interpreting.** The recorded financial data is analysed and interpreted in a manner that the end users can make a meaningful judgement about the profitability and financial health of the business. *Financial ratios* and other techniques are used for the analysis of the financial statements.

5 **Communicating.** The accounting information in the end has to be communicated in a proper form and manner to all the end users. This is done through the preparation and distribution of various *accounting reports.*

The 'accounting process' is presented in Figure 2.3.

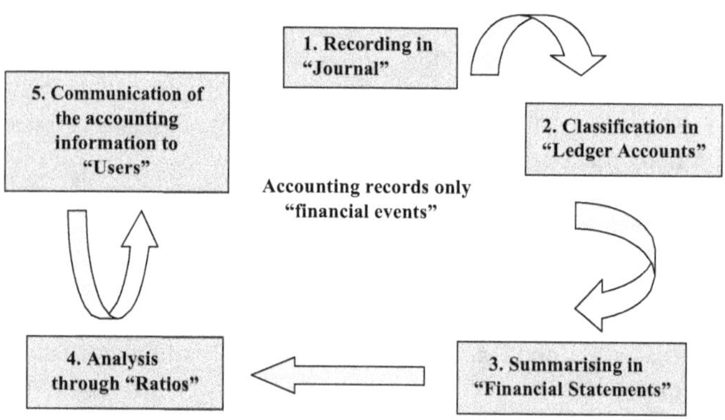

Figure 2.3 Accounting process

3 Understanding of financial statements

The corporate organisations need to regularly update about their business performance to various stakeholders. The source of this data is publicly available reports in the form of 'financial statements'. The profitability and financial strength of the company are ascertained by these financial statements. Their form and content are determined by a set of rules and guidelines known as accounting principles. These financial statements are accessible on company websites, in regulatory filings, financial journals, periodicals and other similar sources.

Financial statements

Financial statements are 'financial reports in a prescribed format required to be prepared by an entity to meet the information needs of various stakeholders'. They commonly include the following:

(a) A 'balance sheet' as at the end of the period (including statement of changes in equity, which is presented as a part of the balance sheet)
(b) A 'statement of profit and loss' for the period
(c) A 'statement of cash flow' for the period
(d) Notes, forming a summary of significant accounting policies and other explanatory information.[1]

DOI: 10.4324/9781003730149-3

Consolidated financial statements

As per Ind AS 110, an entity that is a parent company, in addition to standalone financial statements, shall also *present* 'consolidated financial statements' of the group as a single economic entity.

A parent company shall prepare consolidated financial statements using uniform accounting policies for like transactions and other events in similar circumstances.[2]

Statement of profit and loss

A profit and loss statement or income statement is a summary of an entity's 'result of operations' for a specified period of time. It provides information about the revenue generated and expenses incurred by an organisation during the period. The difference between the revenue and expenses is identified as the 'net profit or net loss'.

An income statement is a flow concept as it reveals the operational performance of a business for the entire period. It relates to the activities for a specified time period (e.g., year, quarter), as clearly noted in the title of the specimen profit and loss statement in Figure 3.1.

Example 3.1

If there are three shirts of Rs. 2,000 each that are sold by a retail outlet during 2023, the offsetting cost of those sales, that is 'cost of goods sold' (COGS), should be recorded as the cost in 2023 that matches the year 2023 sales.

Thus, the cost (at Rs. 1,000 each) of the three shirts sold in 2023 (at Rs. 2,000 each) is taken as the 'cost of goods sold', even though the third shirt was not paid for during the year and will be paid next year.

In other words, the 'matching' principle requires the expenses to be deducted from related revenue in the period in which they occur.

Simply put, the income statement measures all the revenue sources versus business expenses for a given time period.

Statement of Profit and Loss of ABC Ltd. for the year ended 31st March, 2024

(Rs. in crore)

Particulars	Note No.	2023–24	2022–23
REVENUE			
Revenue from operations*	26	63,500	61,500
Other income	27	–	4,000
TOTAL INCOME		63,500	65,500
EXPENSES			
Cost of material consumed		6,000	5,000
Changes in inventories of finished goods, work in progress and scrap	28	–	(2,000)
Employee benefits expense	29	30,000	30,000
Finance costs	30	–	1,000
Depreciation and amortisation expense	31	5,800	5,000
Other expenses	32	14,500	16,000
TOTAL EXPENSES		56,300	55,000
Profit before tax		7,200	10,500
Tax expense	9	3,200	4,500
Profit for the year (Profit after tax – PAT)		**4,000**	**6,000**
Significant accounting policies			
Notes to the financial statements			

Figure 3.1 Statement of profit and loss

Notes:

1. Rs. 1 crore = Rs. 10 million.
2. The profit and loss statement is a specimen statement of a company, ABC Ltd. in the manufacturing sector in India, producing cloth.

To explain the income statement and its components in detail, let's take the example of ABC Ltd.

Revenue from operations (turnover/sales)

'Revenue from operations or sales' refers to what is charged to customers for goods or services. This is the gross revenue generated from the sale of cloth, which is finally adjusted for returns and allowances in the form of discounts given to customers and after *Goods and Services Tax (GST)*. (So, the revenue is Net Revenue.)*

Other income

'Other income' is non-operating income that does not occur during the normal course of business operations. *For instance*, a cloth manufacturer does not normally earn income from the sale of fixed assets or interest on investments, so these income sources are accounted for separately as 'other income'.

> Top line: Turnover and other income are added to determine the 'top line' of the company.

> *For ABC Ltd., the* 'top line' *for 2023–24 is Rs. 63,500 crores as compared to Rs. 65,500 crores of the previous year. It has declined by 3.15% from the previous year, which is a sign of concern for the company.*
>
> *But the positive part is that it has declined not on account of sales but due to non-operating income. Sales have rather shown an increasing trend during the period. The revenue generated from the sale of cloth for 2023–24 is Rs. 63,500 crores. It has increased by 3.25% from the previous year. So, the operating income has shown an increasing trend during the period. This indicates an increase in the core business of the company.*

Operating expenses

'Operating expenses' include production expenses and other operational expenses of the office and selling expenses that are necessary to run the business. They include:

(*i*) *Production expenses.* These are manufacturing expenses incurred in the manufacturing of the product. These costs include material used, direct labour, freight and other costs associated with operating a plant.

(ii) *Office expenses.* These include employee-related and administrative expenses that are incurred in a business. They include:

- *Employee benefits.* It includes salaries of the staff and all benefits given to them in various forms, including provident fund and gratuity.
- *Depreciation.* Depreciation expense is an operating expense because it is incurred on the maintenance and replacement of fixed assets that are used to run the business. It is a non-cash expense in the sense that the cash flows go out only when the asset is purchased, but the cost is taken or charged over period of years of its life, depending on the type of asset. *Its treatment is explained after the* 'balance sheet'.

Finance costs/non-operating expenses

These are considered as non-operating expenses for a non-financing business and include interest on loans, commissions and so forth.

Other expenses

'Other expenses' include those items that are not categorised in the main line of expenses. They range from power and fuel, printing and stationery, insurance and rent to distribution expenses. They are relevant for 'cost control' by the management. They may be operating and/or non- operating in nature.

> *For ABC Ltd., the* 'total expenses' *have increased from Rs. 55,000 crores in 2022–23 to Rs. 56,300 crores in 2023–24, showing an increase of 2.36%. The increase in expenses reduces the net profit of the company.*
>
> *Again, the positive part is that* 'other expenses' *have declined by Rs. 1,500 crores from last year. The increase in total expenses is mainly due to the increase in material consumed of Rs. 1,000 crores. This indicates operational rise for the company.*

Profit before tax/earnings before tax (PBT/EBT)

This figure represents the amount of net income earned by the business before paying taxes.

Income tax

This is the total amount of income taxes paid by the corporate.

Profit after tax (PAT)

This is arrived at after subtracting taxes paid from net income before taxes.

Bottom line: PAT represents the 'bottom line' of the company, that is the net profit left for distribution to shareholders and reinvestment for future growth.

For ABC Ltd., the 'PAT' has declined from Rs. 6,000 crores in 2022–23 to Rs. 4,000 crores in 2023–24. It is a big blow for the company, as it shows a decline of 33.33% in its net profit. This will affect the company's future growth and shareholders' wealth.

Comprehensive income[3]

The statement of profit and loss, besides the net profit or loss, as discussed above, also includes:

1. *Other comprehensive income*: It includes items of income and expense (including reclassification adjustments) that are not recognised in profit or loss as required or permitted by other Ind ASs.
2. *Total comprehensive income*: It is the change in equity during a period resulting from transactions and other

events, other than those changes resulting from transactions with owners in their capacity as owners. Total comprehensive income comprises all components of 'profit or loss' and of 'other comprehensive income'.

Multi-variant statement of profit and loss: the analysis

Financial reporting about the net result of the business to its stakeholders in the form of the profit and loss statement is one dimension of communicating information.

But for better decision-making by the management and other users, the statement of profit and loss is evaluated on a 'multi-variant basis'. This information is generally not reported in the external statement. It helps in evaluating the profitability of the company at various levels in terms of margins for gap analysis and future decision-making.

The above statement of profit and loss of the yarn manufacturer is evaluated on a 'multi-variant basis' as follows.

(i) *Turnover/sales.* 'Sales' refer to what is charged to customers for goods or services. This is the net revenue generated from the sale of cloth, less returns and allowances in the form of discounts given to customers and after GST.

(ii) *Cost of goods sold (COGS).* 'COGS' means the cost, to the company, of the merchandise that is sold to customers. This is the direct cost associated with the manufacturing of cloth at the plant. It is calculated as:

Opening stock + Purchases + Direct expenses (Production exp.) – Closing stock

(iii) *Gross profit.* The gross profit represents the amount of direct profit associated with the actual manufacturing of cloth. It is calculated as:

Gross profit = Sales *less* Cost of goods sold

(iv) *Earnings before interest, tax, depreciation and amortisation* (EBITDA)*. This is the amount of profit earned from the core activities of business, excluding finance cost, tax and depreciation provisioning. It is computed as:

EBITDA = Gross profit *less* Operating expenses (office and selling)

EBITDA is a better indicator to analyse and compare the profitability of similar companies and industries because it eliminates the effects of financing and accounting decisions.

(v) *Earnings before interest and tax (EBIT)/operating profit*. This represents operating profit earned during the normal course of operations after adjusting for non-cash expenses of depreciation and amortisation. It is computed as:

EBIT = EBITDA *less* Depreciation and amortisation

An important factor contributing to the widespread use of EBIT is the way it nulls the effects of the different capital structures and tax rates used by different companies. By excluding both tax and interest expense, the figure measures the company's ability to earn profit and thus makes for easier cross-company comparisons. EBIT is an extension of the EBITDA calculation as it takes the process further by removing non-cash items of depreciation from the equation.

(vi) *Profit before taxes (PBT/EBT)*. This is the amount of profit earned by the business before taxes. It is computed after adjusting non-operating items to the operating profit as follows:

EBT = EBIT *less* Non-operating expenses, like interest paid *Add* Non-operating income, like dividend received

(vii) *Profit after taxes (PAT)*. This is the 'bottom line' (net earnings) of the business. It is computed as:

PAT = EBT *less* Taxes

The above multi-variant profit and loss statement is explained with the help of the following case of ABC Ltd.

Example: Following is the multi-variant income statement of ABC Ltd., given in Figure 3.2.

The above example shows the evaluation of the income statement of ABC Ltd. at various levels as discussed in the preceding section. This is further extended and expressed as a margin with respect to sales for managerial decision-making. **This is explained in detail in the next chapter on** 'Financial Analysis'.

Multi-Step Statement of Profit and Loss of ABC Ltd. for 2023–24	
	(Rs. in crore)
	2023–24
Sales	68,000.00
Less: Cost of production of goods sold (COGS)/Direct Expenses*	10,500.00
Gross Profit – GP	**57,500.00**
Less: Indirect expenses before depreciation, interest & tax	44,500.00
Earnings before Interest, Tax, Depreciation & Amortisation – EBITDA	**13,000.00**
Less: Depreciation	5,800.00
Earnings before Interest and Tax – EBIT	**7,200.00**
Less/Add: Non-Operating Expense (Income)	–
Earnings before Tax – EBT	**7,200.00**
Less: Tax	3,200.00
Profit after Tax – PAT	**4,000.00**

Figure 3.2 Multi-step statement of profit and loss

Note: Rs. 1 crore = Rs. 10 million.

* Direct expenses include GST and the cost of material consumed in Figure 3.1.

** 'Depreciation' is used for the replacement of tangible assets. 'Amortisation' is used for the replacement of intangible assets.

Balance sheet

The balance sheet or position statement is based on the 'accounting equation' and depicts the economic resources owned by an entity and the claims against those resources (liabilities and owner's equity). The balance sheet is prepared on a specific date; that is why it is considered as 'stock' concept.

It presents the 'financial position' of a business in totality, that is it presents the information about the business performance from the day of inception to the date of reporting (including *statement of changes in equity*, which is technically a part of the balance sheet).

Statement of changes in equity[4]

An entity shall present a statement of changes in equity as an extended part of the balance sheet. The statement of changes in equity includes the following information:

(a) Total comprehensive income for the period, showing separately the total amounts attributable to owners of the parent and to non-controlling interests.
(b) For each component of equity, the effects of retrospective application or retrospective restatement.
(c) For each component of equity, a reconciliation between the carrying amount at the beginning and the end of the period.

The specimen balance sheet of ABC Ltd. is given in Figure 3.3.

To explain the balance sheet and its components in detail, let's take the example of ABC Ltd.

Assets side of the balance sheet

On the assets side, the following are included.

1. *Non-current assets*
   These are 'fixed assets' of a tangible and intangible nature.

Balance Sheet of ABC Ltd. as at 31st March, 2024

(Rs. in crore)

Particulars	Note No.	2024	2023
ASSETS			
(1) **Non-Current Assets**			
Property, plant and equipment	1	54,200	53,000
Capital work in progress	2	3,000	1,000
Investment property	3	1,000	1,000
Intangible assets	4	10,000	10,000
Intangible assets under development	5	–	–
Financial assets*	6,7 &8	3,000	2,000
Deferred tax assets	9	700	500
Other non-current assets	10	–	–
		71,900	67,500
(2) **Current Assets**			
Inventories	11	–	2,000
Financial assets			
(i) Trade receivables	12	20,000	25,000
(ii) Cash and cash equivalents	13	1,800	2,000
(iii) Bank balances	14	4,000	3,000
(iv) Loans	7	1,000	–
(v) Other financial assets	15	–	–
Other current assets	16	–	–
		26,800	32,000
TOTAL		98,700	99,500
EQUITY AND LIABILITIES			
EQUITY	17	50,000	50,000
(1) **Equity Share Capital**	18	4,000	6,000
(2) **Other Equity (Reserves and Surplus)**			
		54,000	56,000
LIABILITIES			
(1) **Non-Current Liabilities**			
Financial liabilities**	19 & 20	20,000	20,000
Provisions	21	10,000	10,000
Other non-current liabilities	22	–	–

Figure 3.3 Balance sheet

Notes:

1. Rs. 1 crore = Rs. 10 million.
2. The balance sheet is a specimen statement of a company, ABC Ltd. in the manufacturing sector in India, producing cloth.

* *Financial assets under* 'Non-current assets' *include Investments/Loans/Other financial assets.*

** *Financial liabilities under* 'Non-current liabilities' *include Borrowings/Other financial liabilities.*

Balance Sheet of ABC Ltd. as at 31st March, 2024

(Rs. in crore)

Particulars	Note No.	2024	2023
		30,000	30,000
(2) Current Liabilities			
Financial liabilities			
(i) Trade payables	23	7,000	5,000
(ii) Other financial liabilities	24	4,000	6,000
Other current liabilities	25	–	–
Provisions	21	3,700	2,500
		14,700	13,500
TOTAL		**98,700**	**99,500**
Significant accounting policies			
Notes to the financial statements			

Figure 3.3 (Continued)

(A) PROPERTY, PLANT AND EQUIPMENT
They are composed of the following 'tangible assets', used in business operations.

i. Land
ii. Building
iii. Plant and machinery
iv. Furniture and fixtures
v. Vehicles

(B) CAPITAL WORK IN PROGRESS (CWIP)
This includes under-construction or under-completion of fixed assets, like a building under construction or machinery in transit.

(C) INVESTMENT PROPERTY
This comprises property, kept as an investment by the company.

(D) INTANGIBLE ASSETS
The following are the main items of intangible assets.

i. Goodwill
ii. Patents
iii. Trademarks

iv. Copyrights
v. Licences

(E) INTANGIBLE ASSETS UNDER DEVELOPMENT
This refers to the under-acquisition or process of intangible assets.

(F) FINANCIAL ASSETS
Investment is a financial asset. It is done by the business for getting interest or earning dividend.

The following are the main investments:

i. Investment in government securities
ii. Investment in shares, debentures or bonds

Investment will be shown at cost or market value, whichever is less.

Then, this list also includes loans given to others.

(G) DEFERRED TAX ASSETS
These are fictitious assets and arise as a part of accounting differences between the Companies Act and the Income Tax Act. These could be 'deferred tax liabilities' as well.

(H) OTHER NON-CURRENT ASSETS
This consist of those assets which cannot be categorised above, like securities given.

2. *Current assets*
Current assets are the resources for current usage and consumption. The following components are included here:

(A) INVENTORY

i. Raw material
ii. Work in progress
iii. Finished stock
iv. Stores and spares

(B) FINANCIAL ASSETS
They comprise:

(i) Trade receivables (sundry debtors less provision for doubtful debts)
(ii) Cash in hand and bank balances
(iii) Short-term loans and advances

(C) OTHER CURRENT ASSETS
They are those current assets which cannot be categorised above, like prepaid expenses.

For ABC Ltd., the 'non-current assets' *have increased from Rs. 67,500 crores in 2023 to Rs. 71,900 crores in 2024, showing an increase of 6.52% during the period. The increase is on account of tangible assets property, plant, and equipment (PPE) and capital work in progress. The tangible assets have increased by Rs. 1,200 crores, and CWIP has increased by Rs. 2,000 crores during the period. This is an indication of the growth of the company. Financial assets have also increased by Rs. 1,000 crores during the period, increasing the financial securities base of the company.*

But 'current assets' *have declined from Rs. 32,000 crores in 2023 to Rs. 26,800 crores in 2024. This is mainly due to a decrease in inventories and receivables, indicating a rise in liquidity of the company. Therefore, cash and bank balances of the company have increased from Rs. 5,000 crores in 2023 to Rs. 5,800 crores in 2024.*

The above specimen statement of profit and loss and balance sheet of ABC Ltd. are as per Schedule III of the Indian Companies Act, 2013. Refer to *Schedule III of the Companies Act*, 2013, for specific formats of statement of profit and loss and balance sheet and their contents.

Liabilities side of the balance sheet

In these liabilities, the following are included:

1. *Equity/shareholders' funds*

(A) EQUITY SHARE CAPITAL

The 'equity share capital' of a company represents the funds of a company raised through the issue of ordinary shares, which could be through preference shares as well. It consists of authorised capital, issued capital, subscribed capital and paid-up capital.

(i) The 'authorised share capital' is the maximum limit of capital which the company is registered with the Registrar of Companies to raise.
(ii) The 'issued share capital' can be equal to or lower than authorised capital and represents that amount actually offered to the public for subscription.
(iii) The issued share capital can be under-subscribed or over-subscribed, resulting in the 'subscribed share capital'.
(iv) On subscription, the actual amount paid up by the shareholders is the 'paid-up share capital'.

(B) OTHER EQUITY (RESERVES AND SURPLUS)

This represents the amount of profit undistributed to the shareholders and kept in the form of 'retained earnings'.

The following reserves are shown in the liabilities side of the balance sheet of a company:

i. Capital reserve
ii. Share premium account
iii. General reserve
iv. Other reserves
v. Surplus balance in profit and loss account after providing for dividend

'Net worth': Share capital and reserves and surplus denote the 'net worth' of the company, signifying the shareholders' interest.

For ABC Ltd., the 'net worth' *for 2024 is Rs. 54,000 crores as compared to Rs. 56,000 crores of the previous year, showing a decline of 3.57% from the previous year. A decline in net worth denotes erosion of shareholders' wealth. This decline is due to a decline in profits for the current year.*

2. *Non-current liabilities*

   These represent long-term loans taken by the company. They could be:

(A) FINANCIAL LIABILITIES (BORROWINGS + OTHER FINANCIAL LIABILITIES)

- BORROWINGS – SECURED LOAN

  If any loan is taken by the company against security, then it will be shown under the 'secured loan' head. Its details are given below.

  i. Term loans from banks and financial institutions
  ii. Debentures issued to the banks and financial institutions
  iii. Loan and advances from subsidiaries
  iv. Other loans and advances
  v. Interest payable on secured loan

- BORROWINGS – UNSECURED LOAN

  It is a loan taken by a company without any security. The following are the forms of 'unsecured loan'.

  i. Fixed deposits of the public
  ii. Short-term loans and advances
  iii. Other loans

> *Long-term provisions*: They are kept aside for meeting long-term contingencies and are a part of 'non-current liabilities'.

3. *Current liabilities*

   All liabilities that are payable within one year will be included under the 'current liabilities' head.

(A) FINANCIAL LIABILITIES

These include trade payables/accounts payables and other financial liabilities of short-term borrowings.

(B) OTHER CURRENT LIABILITIES

Other liabilities of short-term nature include acceptance or bill payables and outstanding expenses.

(C) PROVISIONS

i. Provision for taxation
ii. Proposed dividend
iii. Other provisions

For ABC Ltd., the 'non-current liabilities' *have remained constant at Rs. 30,000 crores for the year 2024 from the previous year. This implies there is no change in the long-term financial risk of the company.* 'Current liabilities' *have increased by 9% in 2024 from the previous year. There has been an increase in trade payables during the year by Rs. 2,000 crores, but short-term borrowings have declined by the same amount. This indicates that the company is using bank and vendor management more for short-term financing than long-term borrowings, and this verifies the confidence of banks and vendors in the company. The short-term provisions have increased by Rs. 1,200 crores during the year.*

Depreciation accounting

'In this world, nothing is certain but decline'. This explains the concept of depreciation. The concept of depreciation is not new and was first used by Vitruvius in architecture, 3,820 years ago. The term depreciation was first used in a book of accounting in 1838.

Except land, all fixed assets have a limited period of useful life. If it is assumed that business enterprises acquire assets essentially to earn profits by buying raw materials, merchandise or services (and converting them into finished products or services) and by selling such products or providing such services at a price higher than the cost of purchase or conversion, it would follow that it would be worthwhile for a business enterprise to continue to use an asset only till such time as economic surplus accrues.

Depreciation primarily means 'the reduction in or loss of quality or value of a fixed asset through *physical wear and tear in use* or *passage of time or from any other cause*'. It is very important to make it clear that a fall in value associated with depreciation is necessarily a fall in 'book value'. Therefore, depreciation refers to a fall in the book value, which may or may not be equal to the market value of the asset or the cost price, except in the first year of the life of the asset.

The Institute of Chartered Accountants of India (ICAI) defines **depreciation** as follows:

Depreciation is a measure of the wearing out, consumption or other loss of value of depreciable asset arising from use, effluxion of time or obsolescence through technology and market changes. Depreciation is allocated so as to charge a fair proportion of the depreciable amount in each accounting period during the expected useful life of the asset.

'Depreciation accounting' is the process of writing off the fixed asset during its life and providing funds for its replacement when it becomes unproductive.

According to Committee on Terminology of the American Institute of Certified Public Accountants (AICPA),

> Depreciation accounting is a system of accounting which aims to distribute the cost or other basic value of tangible capital assets, less salvage value (if any), over the estimated useful life of the unit (which may be a group of assets) in a systematic and rational manner. It is a process of allocation not of valuation.

The term 'depreciation' is used for writing off tangible assets, *such as buildings, furniture and machinery.*

'Amortisation' is used for writing off and replacing intangible assets, *like patents, copyrights, trademarks and licences.*

'Depletion' refers to the process of writing off and replacing natural resources, *like coal mines and oil wells.*

Depreciation methods

Various methods of depreciation that are generally used are discussed below.

The two most commonly used methods of depreciation are: *the straight-line method (SLM) and the written-down-value (WDV)** method.

Straight-line method (SLM)

Under the SLM, the depreciation is charged at a fixed amount throughout the life of an asset.

Thus, the amount of depreciation is uniform from year to year. The amount to be written off every year is arrived at as given below:

$$\frac{\textit{Cost} - \textit{Estimated scrap value}}{\textit{Number of years of expected life}}$$

Written-down-value (WDV) method

Under the WDV method, depreciation is charged at a fixed rate on the reducing balance (i.e., cost less depreciation) every year. In other words, depreciation is charged on the net productive value of an asset, which reduces with the usage of an asset.

---

* The SLM is also referred to as the 'fixed instalment method'.

The WDV method is also called the 'diminishing value method' or 'reducing balance method'.

Other depreciation methods

Besides the above, the other 'accelerated depreciation methods'*, including WDV, that are used for calculating depreciation are:

Double declining balance method

Here, the depreciation expense is computed by multiplying the asset cost *less* accumulated depreciation by twice the straight-line rate, expressed as a percentage. No provision is made for the salvage value of the asset.

Sum-of-the-years-digits method

Here, depreciation is calculated by adding up the number of years of the useful economic life; that is, if the asset has an economic useful life of five years, the numbers 1, 2, 3, 4 and 5 are added up. The resulting sum 15 becomes the denominator, while the numerator is the number of remaining years of the useful economic life of the asset.

The formula to be used to calculate depreciation expense here is:

$$\frac{\textit{Remaining years of useful life of the asset(including the beginning of the year)} \times \textit{Original cost of the asset}}{\textit{Sum of the digits of the years of useful life}}$$

The following illustration explains the process of depreciation accounting.

Example 3.2: Young Brothers Ltd., a manufacturing firm, purchases machinery for a sum of Rs. 10,000 on January 1, 2020. They incurred installation charges worth Rs. 1,000 on it. The machinery is depreciated at the rate of 20% per annum and has a useful life of five years.

Compute the necessary depreciation on machinery for five years according to the

1 SLM
2 WDV method

* Accelerated depreciation methods are those that charge relatively greater amounts of depreciation in the early years in the life of the asset and smaller amounts in the later years.

Solution

(a) Effect on Financial Statements – 'SLM'

(In Rs.)

	P/L A/c	*B/S*	
		Accumulated Depreciation	*Net Assets (Net Block)*
2020	2,200	2,200	11,000 – 2,200 = 8,800
2021	2,200	4,400	11,000 – 4,400 = 6,600
2022	2,200	6,600	11,000 – 6,600 = 4,400
2023	2,200	8,800	11,000 – 8,800 = 2,200
2024	2,200	11,000	11,000 – 11,000 = 0

It is clear in the above illustration that in SLM the amount of depreciation remains fixed throughout the life of an asset. At the end of the estimated life, the value of an asset becomes zero.

(b) *Effect on Financial Statements* – 'WDV'

(In Rs.)

	P/L A/c	*B/S*	
		Accumulated Depreciation	*Net Assets (Net Block)*
2020	2,200	2,200	11,000 – 2,200 = 8,800
2021	1,760	3,960	11,000 – 3,960 = 7,040
2022	1,408	5,368	11,000 – 5,368 = 5,632
2023	1,126.40	6,494.40	11,000 – 6,494.40 = 4,505.60
2024	901.12	7,395.52	11,000 – 7,395.52 = 3,604.48

It is clear in the above illustration that in WDV the amount of depreciation does not remain fixed throughout the life of an asset. The depreciation is calculated on the net useful value of the asset.

Cash flow statement

The statement of cash flows describes the enterprise's cash flow position during the time period. It provides the details about how much cash has been generated and expended during a specific period of time from/(on) various sources. It consists of three parts of inflows and outflows resulting from *(a) operating activities, (b) investing activities and (c) financing activities*.

The cash flow statement is a mandatory statement for companies with specified exceptions. Like the income statement, the cash-flow statement measures the financial activity of a firm 'over a period of time'. The cash flow statement also tracks the effects of changes in balance sheet accounts. Ind AS 7, 'Statement of Cash Flows', sets out requirements for the presentation of cash flow information.[5]

The cash flow statement is one of the most useful financial management tools for measuring the liquidity position of the business.

To explain the cash flow statement components in detail and its preparation, let's take the example of ABC Ltd.

Cash flow statement preparation – indirect method

The cash flow statement is divided into three categories:

1 ***Net cash flow from operating activities (CFO).*** Operating activities are the core activities of a business that generate cash and also require cash to carry on. They include cash sales, cash collections from customers, cash paid to suppliers and employees, cash paid for operating expenses and taxes paid.
   Implications: CFO is an indicator of the extent to which the operations of the enterprise have generated cash to meet various operating and other activities.
2 ***Net cash flow from investing activities (CFI).*** Investing activities are discretionary investments made by the management for the future. These primarily consist of the purchase (or sale) of equipment, liquidation (or purchase) of deposits and so forth.
   Implications: CFI is an indicator of the extent to which expenditure has been incurred to generate future income and cash flows.
3 ***Net cash flow from financing activities (CFF).*** Financing activities are fund-related activities, which are either sources or uses of cash and affect cash flow. These include issues of shares, raising of loans, repayments of loans and dividends paid.
   Implications: CFF is useful in finding out the payment and repayment obligations to fund providers.

The sum of **CFO, CFI** and **CFF** is the 'net cash flow'. This could be 'Increase' or 'Decrease' in cash balance. Net cash flow is a very important performance measure as it decides the company's working capital requirements and growth plan.

Steps to calculate CFO

1. Take net profit or loss (before tax) as disclosed by the Statement of P/L.
2. Add:
   (i) *Non-cash items*, like depreciation, amortisation and loss on sale of fixed assets
   (ii) *Non-operating expenses*, like interest paid on loans and financing charges
3. Subtract:
   (iii) *Non-operating income*, like interest received and profit on the sale of fixed assets

---

Operating Profit before Working Capital changes

---

4. Add (inflows)
   (iv) Decrease in 'current assets' and increase in 'current liabilities'
5. Subtract (outflows)
   (v) Increase in 'current assets' and decrease in 'current liabilities'

Notes: Steps 1–3 are calculated using the Statement of P/L.
Steps 4–5 are calculated using the Balance Sheet for Working Capital

(Current Assets versus Current Liabilities)

Steps to calculate CFI and CFF

6. Compare Balance Sheets of two time intervals to find out the increase/decrease in non-current assets and liabilities for investing and financing impact.

Final step to prepare CFS

7. Add CFO + CFI + CFF to get the Change in cash balance as an Increase/Decrease.

Net Increase/Decrease in Cash and Cash Equivalents

The illustrative 'cash flow statement' of ABC Ltd. is given below in Figure 3.4, assuming (a) taxes paid for 2022–23 and 2023–24 are Rs. 4,000 and Rs. 13,000, respectively, and (b) dividends paid during these years are Rs. 5,000 and Rs. 4,000, respectively. *(All other figures, as discussed above, are taken from the Statement of P/L and Balance Sheet.)*

For ABC Ltd., there has not only been a decrease in 'net cash inflow' from Rs. 1,500 crores in 2022–23 to the current year, but there has also been an outflow of Rs. 200 crores in 2023–24. This is despite the CFO being positive and highest. It is a concern for the liquidity position of the company. The major reason has been the dividend pay-out by the company to shareholders, being a family-owned business.

Cash flow from investing activities (CFI) has resulted in an outflow of Rs. 1,200 crores in 2023–24 due to the purchase of fixed assets. Generally, negative cash flow related to investing activities is treated as a sign of growth, due to investment in fixed assets.

Cash flow from financing activities (CFF) has shown an outflow of Rs. 4,000 crores on dividend payment. No interest payment this year indicates leverage-free company.

Cash Flow Statement of ABC Ltd. for the year ended 31st March 2024		
	(Rs. in crore)	
Particulars	2023–24	2022–23
A. CASH FLOW FROM OPERATING ACTIVITIES		
Net Income before tax (as per P/L A/c)	7,200	10,500
Adjustments for:		
(+) Depreciation and Amortisation	5,800	5,000
(-) Interest Income	–	(4,000)
Operating Profit before Working Capital Changes	13,000	11,500
(+) Decrease in Trade Receivables	5,000	(2,000)
(+) Decrease in Inventories	2,000	4,000
(-) Increase in Trade Payables	(2,000)	(1,000)
Cash Generated from Operations	18,000	12,500
Taxes Paid	13,000	4,000
Net Cash from Operating Activities	**5,000**	**8,500**
B. CASH FLOW FROM INVESTING ACTIVITIES		
Sale of Equipment	–	–
Purchase of Equipment	(1,200)	(5,000)
Interest Income	–	4,000
Net Cash used in Investing Activities	**(1,200)**	**(1,000)**
C. CASH FLOW FROM FINANCING ACTIVITIES		
Dividends Paid	(4,000)	(5,000)
Interest Paid	–	(1,000)
Net Cash used in Financing Activities	(4,000)	(6,000)
Net Decrease/Increase in cash and cash equivalents (A+B+C)	(200)	1,500
Opening Balance of Cash and Cash Equivalents	2,000	500
Closing Balance of Cash and Cash Equivalents	1,800	2,000

Figure 3.4 Cash flow statement

Notes:

1. Rs. 1 crore = Rs. 10 million.
2. The above cash flow statement is a specimen statement of a company, ABC Ltd. in the manufacturing sector in India, producing cloth. The above format of cash flow statement is as per the indirect method under 'Ind AS-7'. It is the most common method of preparing the statement by corporate, being based on the income statement.

Other disclosures in the annual report

An annual report, especially of a listed company, is a substantial document. An annual report of a company is not just about financial statements, but it also contains significant information about the company in the form of additional disclosures.

Additional supplemental disclosures provide insights about the related areas of business, as discussed below.

Components of a company's annual report

Chairperson's letter/report. This is given by listed companies and specified public interest entities. The chairperson of the company talks about the challenges and opportunities of the business to the stakeholders of the company for the fiscal year. He/she also shares the achievements, financial highlights and future outlook of the firm.

Board's report. This is a mandatory requirement, though the contents are not standardised. The directors take pleasure in presenting their Report and the Audited Financial Statements for the financial year ended, together with other reports.

Management discussion and analysis report. It is presented by the Chairman or CMD of the company about (a) industry structure and developments, (b) general outlook of the economy, (c) strengths, weaknesses, opportunities and threats and (d) major initiatives undertaken to protect the interests of the company.

Report on corporate governance. This is required for listed companies as per SEBI guidelines. It discusses the philosophy and code of governance adopted by the company, board of directors' details, their remuneration, the board committees and how the company strives to transcend much beyond the basic requirements, focusing towards value addition for all its stakeholders.

Sustainability report. This explains the commitment of the company to achieve the economic, ecological and social responsibility objectives of sustainable development through its varied business operations and activities.

Business responsibility report (BRR). This basically consists of (i) general information about the company, (ii) its financial and other details and (iii) the principle-wise performance of the company.

Independent auditor's report. This is an opinion from the auditors as required by the Companies about auditing the accompanying financial statements of the company.

Notes to accounts. The notes explain the detailed description of items in the statement of profit and loss, the balance sheet and the cash flow statement. In addition, there are notes dealing with matters such as related party transactions.

Accounting policies. In this section of the annual report, the company explains the accounting policies it has used in preparing its accounts. Generally, it contains the basis of measurement that the financial statements are prepared and presented in accordance with the generally accepted accounting principles (GAAP) in India and comprise the mandatory Indian Accounting Standards.

References

1 Indian Accounting Standard (Ind AS 1). www.mca.gov.in/Ministry/pdf/Ind_AS1.pdf (accessed on 7 August 2016).
2 Indian Accounting Standard (Ind AS 110). http://mca.gov.in/Ministry/pdf/INDAS110.pdf (accessed on 7 August 2016).
3 Indian Accounting Standard (Ind AS 1), op. cit.
4 Indian Accounting Standard (Ind AS 1), op. cit.
5 Indian Accounting Standard (Ind AS 7). www.mca.gov.in/Ministry/pdf/Ind_AS7.pdf (accessed on 7 August 2016).

4 Financial analysis for decision-making

Financial analysis establishes relationships between various elements of the financial statements to identify the firm's financial strengths and weaknesses, which is necessary for various stakeholders to make meaningful decisions based on the analysis of financial statements. Financial analysts frequently consider *profitability, liquidity, solvency, efficiency and market performance* when evaluating a particular company. It also entails projecting the business's performance going forward in order to make investment decisions. **This chapter discusses several techniques for analysing financial statements using the manufacturing sector's Maruti Suzuki and Tata Motors as case studies. For the purpose of comparison, other corporate examples from the Indian telecom sector, such as those from the banking and service sectors, which have specific financial ratios, are also being assessed.**

The concept and process of financial analysis

Financial analysis or financial appraisal is 'the process of analysing the financial statements' information of a business organisation at a specific level and interpreting the meaning of those numbers with the help of financial tools'. The financial techniques that are generally used to assign meaning to these numbers include *comparative analysis, common-size analysis, trend analysis and, most importantly,* 'ratio analysis'. 'Ratio analysis' is the most important and widely used technique for financial appraisal.

Comparative analysis is simply comparing the financial statements of the firm at two different intervals or time periods to find out its increasing or declining performance.

DOI: 10.4324/9781003730149-4

Common-size analysis

Common-size analysis is also called 'vertical analysis', as financial statements are analysed on a vertical basis to determine the contribution of each item of the financial statement in total resources or with regard to a common base.

In the case of the *common-size balance sheet*, the contribution of each item is found out in total funds and/or total assets. In the case of the *common-size income statement*, the performance of each element is expressed with 'turnover' as a common base.

Figures 4.1 and 4.2 present the common-size analysis of the balance sheet and income statement.

Rally Industries Ltd.
Common-Size 'Balance Sheet' as at 31st March, 2024

(Rs. in Cr.)

Particulars	2023	2024
ASSETS		
Non-Current Assets		
Property, Plant and Equipment	84,780.38	91,087.99
	(5.84)	(5.99)
Financial Assets	1,198.11	1,911.53
	(0.08)	(0.13)
Deferred Tax Assets	29,949.46	33,779.59
	(2.06)	(2.22)
Other Non-Current Assets	15,657.22	15,089.37
	(1.08)	(0.99)
	131,585.17	141,868.48
	(9.06)	(9.33)

Figure 4.1 Common-size balance sheet

Notes:

* Financial assets are inclusive of trade receivables and cash and bank balances.

** Financial liabilities under 'Current Liabilities' include trade payables and other financial liabilities.

1. Rs. 1 crore = Rs. 10 million.
2. Figures in parentheses show the percentage of each item taking the total funds/ assets as 100.

Particulars	2023	2024
	(Rs. in Cr.)	
Current Assets		
Inventories	329,870.83	336,943.20
	(22.71)	(22.17)
Financial Assets*	869,290.30	966,767.39
	(59.84)	(63.60)
Other Current Assets	121,981.38	74,391.03
	(8.40)	(4.89)
	1,321,142.51	1,378,101.62
	(90.94)	(90.67)
TOTAL	**1,452,727.68**	**1,519,970.10**
	(100.00)	**(100.00)**
EQUITY AND LIABILITIES		
Equity		
Share Capital	8,000.00	8,000.00
	(0.55)	(0.53)
Other Equity (Reserves & Surplus)	694,985.02	781,413.40
	(47.84)	(51.41)
	702,985.02	789,413.40
	(48.39)	(51.94)
Liabilities		
Non-Current Liabilities		
Financial Liabilities	694.61	107.57
	(0.05)	(0.007)
Provisions	35,618.95	43,328.96
	(2.45)	(2.85)
	36,313.56	43,436.53
	(2.50)	(2.86)

Figure 4.1 (Continued)

Particulars	(Rs. in Cr.) 2023	2024
Current Liabilities		
Financial Liabilities**	119,705.91	112,614.00
	(8.24)	(7.41)
Other Current Liabilities	569,393.54	540,167.59
	(39.19)	(35.54)
Provisions	24,329.65	34,338.58
	(1.67)	(2.26)
	713,429.10	687,120.17
	(49.11)	(45.21)
TOTAL	**1,452,727.68**	**1,519,970.10**
	(100.00)	(100.00)

Figure 4.1 (Continued)

Rally Industries Ltd.
Common-Size 'Profit & Loss' for the year ended 31st March, 2024

Particulars	(Rs. in Cr.) 2022–23	2023–24
REVENUE		
Revenue from operations (Net)	**612,228.16**	**667,553.84**
	(100.00)	(100.00)
Other income	42,847.44	47,795.18
	(7.00)	(7.16)
TOTAL REVENUE	655,075.60	715,349.02

Figure 4.2 Common-size income statement

Notes:

1. Rs. 1 crore = Rs. 10 million.
2. Figures in parentheses show the percentage of each item taking the net turnover (revenue from operations) as 100.

Particulars	(Rs. in Cr.) 2022–23	2023–24
EXPENSES		
Cost of Material Consumed	310,938.06	326,534.05
	(50.79)	(48.92)
Changes in Inventories of Finished Goods, WIP & Scrap	4,733.28	3,602.18
	(0.77)	(0.54)
Employee Benefits Expense	103,042.56	126,345.08
	(16.83)	(18.93)
Finance Costs	339.61	138.38
	(0.06)	(0.02)
Depreciation and Amortisation Expense	14,210.45	15,396.49
	(2.32)	(2.31)
Other Expenses	72,308.59	65,531.99
	(11.81)	(9.82)
TOTAL EXPENSES	505,572.55	537,548.17
	(82.58)	(80.53)
Profit for the period before tax	149,503.05	177,800.85
	(24.42)	(26.63)
Tax Expense	24,311.77	29,944.58
	(3.97)	(4.49)
Profit for the year after tax (PAT)	**125,191.28**	**147,856.27**
	(20.45)	**(22.15)**

Figure 4.2 (Continued)

Analysis

ASSET STRUCTURE

The share of investment in 'total fixed assets' has increased from 9.06% in 2023 to 9.33% in 2024. The net block (PPE) has shown an increasing trend from 5.84% in 2023 to 5.99% in 2024.

Similarly, the percentage share of financial assets (long-term investments) in total assets has also shown an increasing trend during the period. So, the position of investment in fixed assets can be categorised as satisfactory.

The level of 'working capital' has also registered quite a stable trend during the period. The level of inventories is almost constant, and financial assets including trade receivables and cash and bank balances have resulted in an increasing trend by around 4%. This shows better liquidity of the company.

FINANCIAL STRUCTURE

It is clear from the above that the company's 'net worth' has gone up from 48.39% in 2023 to 51.94% in 2024, an increase of 3.6% during the period under study. It is on account of reserves and surplus, which is a good sign for shareholders' interest in the company.

'Loan funds' of the company have decreased from 0.05% in 2023 to 0.007% in 2024. 'Trade payables and other current liabilities' have also shown a decreasing trend as a percentage share during the period. On the whole, the firm's dependence on borrowed capital has decreased. This is a sound affair, particularly from the point of view of stability of the concern.

Analysis

From the analysis of the common-size income statement of Rally Industries, it is evident that at an absolute level, the total expenses have shown an increasing figure from Rs. 505,572.55 cr. in 2023 to Rs. 537,548.17 cr. in 2024. But margin-wise, the company has been able to tighten its expenses by over 2%, though not much, during the period. This is mainly due to a reduction in finance costs. Other expenses have also gone down by 2%. This is a positive sign as it has resulted in an increasing profit margin for the company.

Trend analysis

It is used to determine the growth pattern of a company. Here, the base year is taken as 100, and the respective years are expressed in percentage to find out the growth trend. In

Table 4.1 Samy Industries Ltd. Trend Analysis (2017–18 to 2021–22) (Rs. in Cr.)

	2017–18	*2018–19*	*2019–20*	*2020–21*	*2021–22*
Results for the Year					
Sales/Turnover	73,164	89,124	118,354	139,269	146,328
Index	100	122	162	190	200
Earnings before interest, tax, dep. & amort. (EBITDA)	14,261	14,982	20,525	23,130	19,960
Index	100	105	144	162	140
Profit after tax (PAT)	7,572	9,069	11,943	19,458	15,309
Index	100	120	158	257	202
Dividend payout	1,045	1,393	1,440	1,631	1,898
Index	100	133	138	156	182
Position at the Year End					
Total assets	59,955	91,928	107,061	104,229	149,628
Index	100	153	179	174	250
Net worth	40,403	49,804	63,967	81,449	126,373
Index	100	123	158	202	313

Table 4.1, 2017–18 of Samy Industries Ltd. is taken as the 'base year' to which the coming years' financials of the income statement and position statement are converted into percentages for studying the trend.

Figure 4.3 shows the graphical presentation of the trend analysis of results of the company.

Analysis

It is evident from the above trend analysis that the company has been experiencing an increasing trend in sales during these years; the absolute figures indicate that the company's sales have doubled from Rs. 73,164 cr. in 2018 to Rs. 146,328 cr. in 2022. This indicates a tightening market grip and is a good sign for the long-term growth of the company. A similar trend is evident in its EBITDA figures, except in 2021–22.

Again, at an absolute level, the PAT of the company has been showing a continuous increasing trend and more than doubled up during the period. But its current year trend is lower than the last year, which reflects a declining yearly margin.

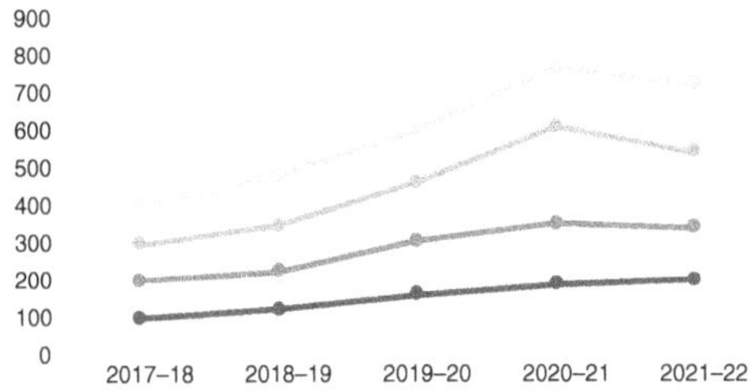

	2017–18	2018–19	2019–20	2020–21	2021–22
Dividend payout	100	133	138	156	182
Profit after tax (PAT)	100	120	158	257	202
Earnings before interest, tax, dep. & amort. (EBITDA)	100	105	144	162	140
Sales/Turnover	100	122	162	190	200

Figure 4.3 Trend graph

Ratio analysis

Ratio analysis is the most important tool used in the financial analysis of a firm. It involves computing 'financial ratios' and analysing the business performance based on them. A 'financial ratio' is a relationship between two financial elements that indicates information about business activities, such as the ratio between a company's current assets and its current liabilities, which indicates its liquidity position. The basic source of these ratios is the company's financial statements.

These ratios enable the identification of the financial strengths and weaknesses of a company at an intrinsic level. When assessing ratios, it is important that the results are compared with other companies in the same industry and not taken in isolation. What may seem like a poor ratio at first glance may well be normal for that industry, and of course, the reverse applies, in that what may seem a good ratio on its own could be below average for that industry.

The following is the discussion on various types of financial ratios that are used for analysis.

- Profitability ratios
- Operating efficiency ratios/turnover ratios
- Liquidity ratios
- Solvency ratios
- Market performance ratios

Financial ratios and their usage

Profitability ratios – the overall performance of t/he firm and its return generation.
Efficiency ratios – the efficiency of managing assets/ resources.
Liquidity ratios – the firm's ability to meet cash needs as they arise.
Solvency ratios – the extent of a firm's financing with debt relative to equity and its ability to cover fixed charges.
Market ratios – the firm's financial market(s) standing for shareholders.

Profitability ratios

These ratios are used to analyse the profitability of a company in total and the return generated for shareholders. They help in determining the profit capacity of the firm at different levels. That's why there are several measures to analyse the success of the firm in generating profits.

These are:

- *sales-based ratios* (sales are taken as 'net sales')
- *assets/funds-based ratios*

SALES-BASED PROFITABILITY RATIOS

1. *Gross profit ratio.* The gross profit ratio or the gross profit margin indicates the margin generated out of sales after meeting 'production expenses' of raw material, labour and so forth. The higher the value of the margin, the better it is for the firm.

$$\text{Gross Profit Ratio} = \frac{\text{Gross Profit}}{\text{Sales}}$$

$(Gross\ Profit = Sales - COGS^{*})$

Example

Right Ltd. earned Rs. 10,000 from the sale of readymade garments. The production expenses incurred are Rs. 4,000.

Its gross profit margin would be 60%. It means that for every rupee earned on sale, it has Rs. 0.60 left for meeting other expenses.

2. *EBITDA margin.* EBITDA margin measures the profitability of a concern after meeting other line of operating expenses out of sales, after production expenses. The other operating expenses include office and selling expenses but exclude non-cash expenses of depreciation and provisions.

$$\text{EBITDA Ratio} = \frac{\text{EBITDA}^{**}}{\text{Sales}}$$

(*EBITDA = Gross Profit – Other Operating expenses*)

EBITDA margin determines the core strength of the company as it excludes non-operating items and taxes**σ. The higher the margin, the better it is.

Example

In the above example, let's assume administrative expenses are Rs. 2,000. Marketing expenses including freight on sales of goods are Rs. 1,000.

The EBITDA amount would be: Rs. 3,000 (Rs. 6,000 – Rs. 3,000). The EBITDA margin is 30%. This implies that 30% is left out for meeting depreciation, interest and tax expenses.

From a gross margin of 60%, office and selling expenses have consumed another 30% of profit.

3. *Operating profit ratio/EBIT margin.* Operating profit margin measures the profitability of a concern after charging the non-cash expense of depreciation out of EBITDA.

$$\text{Operating Profit Ratio} = \frac{\text{EBIT}^{***}/\text{Operating Profit}}{\text{Sales}}$$

(*Operating Profit = EBITDA – Depreciation*)

** EBITDA = Earnings before interest, tax, depreciation and amortisation.

**σ For detailed discussion on EBITDA, refer to the section 'Multi-Variant Profitability' in Chapter 3, 'Understanding of Financial Statements'.

*** EBIT = Earnings before interest and tax.

'EBITDA and EBIT': Both EBITDA and EBIT margin determine the core strength of the company as they exclude non-operating items and taxes. They are an expression of 'the operating profit' of the firm.***σ

The difference between EBITDA and EBIT is of 'depreciation and amortisation'.

The higher the operating profit margin, the better it is.

Example

Taking the above example further, if the depreciation amount is Rs. 1,000, the operating profit would be Rs. 2,000 (Rs. 3,000 – Rs. 1,000).

The operating profit margin is 20%. This signifies that depreciation has consumed 10% of profit from the EBITDA margin of 30%, and the remaining 20% will be used for meeting interest and taxes.

4. *Net profit ratio/PAT margin.* The net profit margin measures the net margin of profitability on sales. It indicates how much of each rupee earned by the company is finally translated into profits. Therefore, this is the net indicator for measuring the efficiency of operations and the best indicator of the business's ability to face all pressures. A higher net profit margin is always desirable.

$$\text{Net Profit Ratio} = \frac{\text{PAT}}{\text{Sales}}$$

5. *Operating ratio.* The operating ratio analyses the profitability of the firm with regard to the coverage of expenses. 'Unlike the above profitability ratios, this ratio should be as low as possible'. The lower the ratio, the greater the organisation's ability to generate profits if revenues decrease.

$$\text{Operating Ratio} = \frac{\text{Total Operating Expenses}}{\text{Sales}}$$

***σ For detailed discussion on operating profit, refer to the section 'Multi-Variant Profitability' in Chapter 3, 'Understanding of Financial Statements'.

ASSETS/FUNDS-BASED PROFITABILITY RATIOS

1. *Return on investment/return on capital employed.* Return on investment (ROI) is also commonly used as return on capital employed (ROCE). It measures whether or not a company is generating adequate profits in relation to the funds invested in it and is a key indicator of investment performance. In the 'manufacturing sector', figures are expected in excess of 10% rising to over 25% at the top end. In the 'retail sector', lower figures would be experienced, ranging between 5% and 15%.

'Construction sector' figures show an average of about 7% increasing to over 35% for the top performers.

$$\text{Return on Investment (ROI)} = \frac{\text{EBIT}}{\text{Investment}}$$

or

$$\text{Return on Capital Employed (ROCE)} = \frac{\text{EBIT}}{\text{Capital Employed}}$$

(Capital Employed = Net worth + Preference Share Capital + Long-term Loans)

2. *Return on equity.* Return on equity or return on net worth (ROE/RONW) is a very important ratio for equity shareholders as it indicates whether or not a company is generating enough return for them. ROE is an indicator of how effectively a company's management uses owners' money. It calculates the amount of net income returned as a percentage of equity shareholders.
   Higher return on equity is always favourable as it indicates the efficiency of a company in converting the shareholders' capital to profits.

$$\text{Return on Equity (ROE)} = \frac{\text{PAT} - \text{Preference dividend}}{\text{Net Worth}}$$

Net Worth = Equity Share Capital + Other Equity (Reserves and Surplus)

3. *Earnings per share.* Earnings per share (EPS) is defined as the portion of a company's profit allocated to each outstanding share of a common stock. Higher EPS signifies better profitability from a shareholder's point of view.

$$\text{Earnings per Share (EPS)} = \frac{\text{PAT} - \text{Preference Dividend}}{\text{Number of Equity Shares}}$$

Example

A company earned a net profit of Rs. 50,000 for 2022. It has 1,000 outstanding equity shares. There are no preference shares.

So, EPS = 50,000/1,000
= Rs. 50

4. *Dividend per share.* Dividend per share (DPS) is defined as the portion of a company's net profit distributed to each common shareholder. Higher DPS indicates that company is cash-rich and looks after the equity shareholders well.

$$\text{Dividend per Share (DPS)} = \frac{\text{Dividend paid to Equity Shareholders}}{\text{Number of Equity Shares}}$$

Example

Taking the above example, the company paid a dividend of Rs. 10,000 from the net profit of Rs. 50,000 for 2022. It has 1,000 outstanding equity shares.

So, DPS = 10,000/1,000
= Rs. 10

5. *Dividend pay-out ratio.* The dividend pay-out ratio (D/P ratio) refers to the amount of dividend paid per share with respect to the EPS. It denotes the percentage of earnings distributed as dividends to the common shareholders.

$$\text{Dividend Pay-out Ratio (D/P Ratio)} = \frac{\text{DPS}}{\text{NPS}}$$

In the *above example,*
D/P ratio will be 10/50 = 20%

Profitability ratios: *All profitability ratios, except EPS and DPS, are expressed as a* 'percentage'. *EPS and DPS are expressed in* 'rupees per share'.

ROE – DuPont analysis: shareholders' wealth maximisation (SWM)

The ultimate objective of a company is to 'maximise shareholders' value'. ROE shows the rate of return that the firm earns on stockholders' equity. DuPont analysis is used to find out the factors responsible for the performance of shareholders' value in terms of 'ROE'. In short, it is used to analyse the shareholders' wealth maximisation (SWM). If ROE is unsatisfactory, the DuPont analysis helps to locate the part of the business that is underperforming.

DuPont analysis is a method of performance analysis started by the DuPont Corporation in the USA in the 1920s. It evaluates the ROE effect on three variables:

1 *Profitability,* measured by the 'net profit margin'
2 *Assets' efficiency,* measured by the 'total assets turnover'
3 *Financial leverage,* measured by the 'equity multiplier'

It is known that, ROE = PAT/shareholders' equity

In DuPont, ROE is further subdivided into the following ratios for studying in depth the focus areas for performance of shareholders' value:

ROE = PAT Margin × Total Assets Turnover × Equity Multiplier

Thus, ROE = PAT/Sales × Sales/Total Assets × Total Assets/Shareholders' equity

DuPont Analysis of the Indian fast-moving consumer goods (FMCG) sector!

In the Indian FMCG sector, 'ROE' performance of the top ten companies is analysed with the help of the DuPont model to find out whether these companies contribute to shareholders' wealth or not? These companies are chosen based on their market capitalisation as of June 10, 2013.

The financials of the companies have been taken from their annual reports. These corporations are multinational corporations (MNCs), so their analysis will be useful for the global community.

The DuPont analysis of these companies is given in Table 4.2.

RANKING AND WEIGHT BASED ON THE DUPONT SCORES

The companies were ranked on each of the four scores (in two decimals), and a weight was assigned to them based on their ranking.

Table 4.2 Competitive DuPont analysis of FMCG companies for 2012

Rank	*Name*	*Market capitalisation (Rs. in crores)*	*Net profit margin (%)*	*Total assets turnover*	*Equity multiplier*	*ROE (%)*
1	ITC	1,51,078	24	0.69	2.01	33
2	HUL	67,858	12	2.12	3.12	79
3	Nestle India	39,819	13	1.62	2.87	60
4	Dabur	18,632	12	1.32	2.18	35
5	GCPL	13,335	19	0.87	1.42	23
6	CP*	12,764	16	2.42	2.59	100
7	GSKCH**	9,842	16	1.05	1.88	32
8	P&G	9,778	14	1.49	1.26	26
9	Marico	9,078	8	1.52	2.29	29
10	Emami	6,836	18	1.26	1.66	38

Source: Companies' Annual Reports

Notes:
* Colgate-Palmolive
** Glaxo SmithKline
1. Rs. 1 crore = Rs. 10 million

Rank as per Market Cap	*Company*	*Ranking as per Net Profit Margin*	*Ranking as per Total Assets Turnover*	*Ranking as per Equity Multiplier*	*Ranking as per ROE*	*Total Score*
1	ITC	1	10	6	6	23
2	HUL	9	2	1	2	14
3	Nestle India	7	3	2	3	15
4	Dabur	8	6	5	5	24
5	GCPL	2	9	9	10	30
6	**CP**	**5**	**1**	**3**	**1**	**10**
7	GSKCH	4	8	7	7	26
8	P&G	6	5	10	9	30
9	Marico	10	4	4	8	26
10	Emami	3	7	8	4	22

Analysis

- It can be inferred that Colgate-Palmolive, although sixth in the ranking as per market capitalisation, ranks the highest in terms of 'shareholders' wealth maximisation' with the highest ROE, though it has the lowest score (rank). It is an ideal investment for shareholders even during weak market conditions.
- It is clear that FMCG companies are usually zero-/low-debt companies with high reserves and surplus. They are growth companies and hence are stable companies. Therefore, they are considered ideal for long-term investment by shareholders.

Financial analysis of Maruti Suzuki and Tata Motors

The 'financial statements' of leading companies in the Indian automobile sector, 'Maruti Suzuki India Ltd. (MSIL)' and 'Tata Motors Ltd. (TML)' from 2018–19 to 2021–22, are given in Tables 4.3–4.6. They are analysed here in the subsequent section(s) on the given parameters of financial analysis for applied learning. Both these companies are MNCs and have global presence, which makes the analysis relevant at the international level. Further, both are listed in BSE (Bombay Stock Exchange) Limited and NSE (National Stock Exchange) Limited, India's leading stock exchanges.

INDIAN AUTOMOBILE SECTOR

The Indian automobile industry has historically been a good indicator of how well the economy is doing, as the automobile sector plays a key role in both macroeconomic expansion and technological advancement. The Auto industry includes commercial vehicles, passenger vehicles and utility vehicles. India's annual production of automobiles in FY22 was 22.93 million vehicles.[1]

MSIL is the Indian subsidiary of Japanese automaker Suzuki Motor Corporation. The company is known for making highly reliable, low-maintenance cars for the Indian market. The company was instated as Maruti Udyog Limited (MUL) in February 1981, and it has been the market leader since its inception.

Table 4.3 Balance sheets of MSIL from 2019 to 2022

	(Rs. in Millions)			
	Mar' 19	*Mar' 20*	*Mar' 21*	*Mar' 22*
ASSETS:				
Non-current assets				
Property, plant and equipment	149,567	147,618	741,511	127,995
Capital work in progress	16,001	13,374	11923	26,391
Intangible assets*	4,511	10,914	11,034	12,081
Financial assets	314,037	352,848	334,075	367,004
Non-current tax assets	–	–	–	5,429
Deferred tax assets	–	–	–	2,027
Other non-current assets	20,586	17,213	16,864	25,204
Total	**505,702**	**541,247**	**515,407**	**566,131**
Current assets				
Inventories	33,257	32,149	30,500	35,331
Financial assets				
Investments	50,455	12,188	84,157	41,001
Trade receivables	23,104	21,270	12,766	20,301
Cash and bank balances	1,789	212	30,364	30,362
Loans	160	169	230	305
Other financial assets	4,964	5,075	6,410	25,892
Current tax assets	4,274	5,269	5,396	–

(Continued)

Table 4.3 (Continued)

	(Rs. in Millions)			
	Mar' 19	*Mar' 20*	*Mar' 21*	*Mar' 22*
Other current assets	5,613	7,943	15,444	14,620
Total	**123,616**	**84,274**	**185,267**	**167,812**
TOTAL ASSETS	**629,318**	**625,521**	**700,674**	**733,943**
EQUITY AND LIABILITIES				
Equity				
Equity share capital	1,510	1,510	1,510	1,510
Other equity (R&S)	459,905	482,860	512,158	539,350
Total	**461,415**	**484,370**	**513,668**	**540,860**
Liabilities				
Non-current liabilities				
Financial liabilities	–	550	353	302
Provisions	395	516	447	833
Deferred tax liabilities	5,640	5,984	3,847	–
Other non-current liabilities	20,365	21,153	21,292	21,811
Total	**26,400**	**28,203**	**25,939**	**22,946**

(Continued)

Table 4.3 (Continued)

	(Rs. in Millions)			
	Mar' 19	*Mar' 20*	*Mar' 21*	*Mar' 22*
Current liabilities				
Financial liabilities				
Borrowings	1,496	1,063	4,888	3,819
Trade payables	96,330	74,941	101,617	97,610
Other financial liabilities**	14,400	9,111	12,758	20,312
Provisions	6,244	6,796	7,416	8,613
Current tax liabilities	6,729	6,962	8,539	11,104
Other current liabilities	16,304	14,075	25,849	28,679
Total	**141,503**	**112,948**	**161,067**	**170,137**
TOTAL EQUITY AND LIABILITIES	**629,318**	**625,521**	**700,674**	**733,943**

Source: Annual Reports of MSIL

Notes:

* Intangible assets include intangible assets under development and right-of-use assets.

** Other financial liabilities are inclusive of lease liabilities.

Table 4.4 Statements of profit and loss of MSIL from 2019 to 2022

	(Rs. in Millions)			
	Mar' 19	*Mar' 20*	*Mar' 21*	*Mar' 22*
INCOME:				
Revenue from operations	860,203	750,106	703,325	882,956
Other income	25,610	34,208	29,464	17,935
Total Income	**885,813**	**790,314**	**732,789**	**900,891**
EXPENSES:				
Cost of materials consumed	450,239	346,366	332,969	397,387
Purchase of stock-in-trade	150,195	187,581	172,472	263,905
Changes in inventories	2,108	(2,381)	2,731	(919)
Employee benefits expense	32,549	33,839	34,029	40,222
Finance costs	758	1,329	1,008	1,259
Depreciation and Amortisation expense	30,189	35,257	30,315	27,865
Other expenses*	115,119	117,675	107,671	125,349
Total expenses	**781,157**	**719,666**	**681,195**	**855,068**
Profit/(Loss) before tax	104,656	70,648	51,594	45,823
Tax expense	29,650	14,142	9,297	8,160
Profit/(Loss) after tax (PAT)	**75,006**	**56,506**	**42,297**	**37,663**

(*Continued*)

Table 4.4 (Continued)

	(Rs. in Millions)			
	Mar' 19	*Mar' 20*	*Mar' 21*	*Mar' 22*
EBITDA	109,993	67,026	53,453	57,012
EBIT/Operating Profit	79,804	31,769	23,138	29,147
Earnings per share (Rs.)	248.30	187.06	140.02	124.68

Source: Annual Reports of MSIL

Notes:
* Other expenses include vehicles/dies for own use.
1. EBITDA (Sales – Exp. excld. Int., Tax & Dep.)
2. EBIT/Operating Profit (EBITDA – Dep.)
3. Earnings per share/EPS (Rs.) = PAT/Number of equity shares

Table 4.5 Balance sheets of TML from 2019 to 2022

	(Rs. in Crores)			
	Mar' 19	*Mar' 20*	*Mar' 21*	*Mar' 22*
ASSETS:				
Non-current assets				
Property, plant and equipment	18,317	18,871	19,153	11,733
Capital work in progress	2,147	1,756	1,401	585
Intangible assets*	8,110	9,077	8,875	3,224
Investments in subsidiaries, JVs & associates	14,771	15,182	15,147	27,917
Financial assets	1,801	2,200	2,725	3,380
Non-current tax assets	715	728	715	778
Other non-current assets	1,820	1,208	1,187	662
Total	**47,680**	**49,021**	**49,205**	**48,280**
Current assets				
Inventories	4,662	3,832	4,552	3,718
Investments in subsidiaries & associates	258	–	–	–
Financial assets				
Investment	1,175	885	1,578	5,143
Trade receivables	3,251	1,978	2,088	2,112
Cash and bank balances	1,307	3,532	4,319	2,605
Loans and advances	200	232	185	139
Other financial assets	1,280	1,547	1,745	810

(Continued)

Table 4.5 (Continued)

	(Rs. in Crores)			
	Mar' 19	*Mar' 20*	*Mar' 21*	*Mar' 22*
Assets held-for-sale	162	191	221	–
Other current assets	935	1,372	1,167	1,092
Total	**13,229**	**13,569**	**15,855**	**15,620**
TOTAL ASSETS	60,910	62,590	65,060	63,900
EQUITY AND LIABILITIES				
Equity				
Equity share capital	679	720	766	766
Other equity (R&S)	21,483	17,668	18,290	19,178
Total	**22,163**	**18,388**	**19,056**	**19,944**
Liabilities				
Non-current liabilities				
Financial liabilities	14,101	16,153	17,580	14,801
Provisions	1,282	1,770	1,372	1,474
Deferred tax liabilities	206	199	267	174
Other non-current liabilities	218	270	534	514
Total	**15,806**	**18,391**	**19,752**	**16,963**

(*Continued*)

Table 4.5 (Continued)

	(Rs. in Crores)			
	Mar' 19	*Mar' 20*	*Mar' 21*	*Mar' 22*
Current liabilities				
Financial liabilities				
Borrowings	3,618	6,121	2,543	9,130
Lease liabilities-	–	83	96	59
Trade payables**	13,502	10,844	15,988	13,986
Other financial liabilities	2,238	5,976	4,256	1,113
Provisions	1,149	1,407	1,044	608
Current tax liabilities	78	31	38	50
Other current liabilities	2,356	1,348	2,288	2,047
Total	**22,941**	**25,811**	**26,252**	**26,993**
TOTAL EQUITY AND LIABILITIES	**60,910**	**62,590**	**65,060**	**63,900**

Source: Annual Reports of TML

Notes:
* Intangible assets include goodwill, etc., other intangible assets & intangible assets under development.
** Trade payables consist of acceptances as well.
1. Rs. 1 crore = Rs. 10 million.

Table 4.6 Statements of profit and loss of TML from 2019 to 2022(Rs. in Crores)

	(Rs. in Crores)			
	Mar' 19	*Mar' 20*	*Mar' 21*	*Mar' 22*
INCOME:				
Revenue from operations	69,203	43,928	47,031	47,264
Other income	2,555	1,383	843	660
Total Income	**71,757**	**45,311**	**47,874**	**47,924**
EXPENSES:				
Cost of materials consumed	43,749	26,172	30,011	31,693
Purchase of products for sale	6,722	5,680	5,491	5,030
Changes in inventories	145	723	(69)	(404)
Employee benefits expense	4,273	4,384	4,213	3,602
Finance costs	1,794	1,973	2,359	2,122
Foreign exchange loss	215	239	2	137
Depreciation and Amortisation expense	3,099	3,375	3,682	1,761
Product development/Engineering Expenses	572	830	908	594
Other expenses	9,680	7,721	5,802	6,019
Amount transferred to capital and other accounts	(1,093)	(1,169)	(818)	(905)
Total expenses	**69,155**	**49,928**	**51,579**	**49,647**
Profit/(Loss) before Exceptional items & tax	2,602	(4,616)	(3,705)	(1,723)
Exceptional items	203	2,511	(1,392)	(83)

(*Continued*)

Table 4.6 (Continued)

	(Rs. in Crores)			
	Mar' 19	*Mar' 20*	*Mar' 21*	*Mar' 22*
Profit/(Loss) before tax	2,399	(7,127)	(2,313)	(1,640)
Tax expense	378	162	83	99
Profit/(Loss) after tax (PAT)	**2,021**	**(7,290)**	**(2,395)**	**(1,739)**
EBITDA	4,062	(1,582)	675	730
EBIT/Operating Profit	963	(4,957)	(3,007)	(1,031)
Earnings per share (Rs.)	5.94	(21.06)	(6.59)	(3.63)

Source: Annual Reports of TML

Notes:
1. Rs. 1 crore = Rs. 10 million.
2. EBITDA (Sales – Exp. excld. Int., Tax & Dep.)
3. EBIT/Operating Profit (EBITDA – Dep.)
4. Earnings per share/EPS (Rs.) = PAT/Number of equity shares

Table 4.7 Sales-based profitability

	Mar' 19	*Mar' 20*	*Mar' 21*	*Mar' 22*
(i) **EBITDA Margin** (%)				
MSIL	12.79	8.94	7.60	6.46
TML	5.87	3.60	1.44	1.54
Industry	12.07	9.40	9.57	9.44
(ii) **EBIT Margin** (%)				
MSIL	9.28	4.24	3.29	3.30
TML	1.39	-11.28	-6.39	-2.18
Industry	8.24	4.76	4.43	5.16
(iii) **Net Profit Margin** (%)				
MSIL	8.72	7.53	6.01	4.27
TML	2.92	-16.60	-5.09	-3.68
Industry	5.70	1.80	2.26	3.51

Note: Automobile industry figures are taken from the 'Capitaline' *(https://awsone.capitaline.com)* database.

TML is an Indian multinational automotive manufacturing company, headquartered in Mumbai, India, which is part of the Tata Group. The company produces passenger cars, trucks, vans, coaches and buses.

Profitability analysis of Maruti Suzuki and Tata Motors

The analysis of profitability on the above parameters of the companies under study is given in Tables 4.7–4.10.

Analysis

- The operating profit margin and net profit margin for MSIL and TML have shown a declining trend during the period under study due to the natural calamity of COVID, except for TML in the current year 2022.
- Both EBITDA and EBIT margins of MSIL are higher than TML. This is a positive sign for the company.

- MSIL in terms of PAT margin wins over not only TML but also its peers in the Indian automobile industry. It is much higher for MSIL, which indicates that TML must be losing out on account of non-operating expenses and other items. Thus, MSIL is a greater profit-making company as compared to TML in the ultimate, including its core efficiency.

'Return generation and ROE efficiency' of the units are discussed in Table 4.8. This is further analysed with the help of the DuPont analysis as given in Tables 4.9 and 4.10. The graphical representation of the DuPont analysis is given in Figures 4.4 and 4.5.

Table 4.8 Assets-based profitability

	Mar' 19	*Mar' 20*	*Mar' 21*	*Mar' 22*
(i) **Return on Investment** – **ROI** (%)				
MSIL	16.36	6.20	4.29	5.17
TML	2.54	-13.48	-7.75	-2.79
Industry	15.39	7.77	6.80	9.56
(ii) **Return on Equity** – **ROE/RONW** (%)				
MSIL	16.26	11.67	8.23	6.96
TML	9.12	-39.65	-12.57	-8.72
Industry	13.92	3.84	4.63	8.55

Note: Automobile industry figures are taken from the 'Capitaline' *(https://awsone.capitaline.com)* database.

Table 4.9 DuPont analysis of Maruti Suzuki (MSIL)

	Mar' 19	*Mar' 20*	*Mar' 21*	*Mar' 22*
(1) PAT/Sales (%) – 'Net Profit Margin'	8.72	7.53	6.01	4.27
(2) Sales/Total Assets (times) – 'Assets Turnover Ratio'	1.37	1.20	1.00	1.20
(3) Total Assets/Shareholders' equity (times) – 'Assets to Equity Ratio'	1.36	1.29	1.36	1.36
1 × 2 × 3 = ROE (%)	16.26	11.67	8.23	6.96

Table 4.10 DuPont analysis of Tata Motors (TML)

	Mar' 19	*Mar' 20*	*Mar' 21*	*Mar' 22*
(1) PAT/Sales (%) – 'Net Profit Margin'	2.92	–16.60	–5.09	–3.68
(2) Sales/Total Assets (times) – 'Assets Turnover Ratio'	1.14	0.70	0.72	0.74
(3) Total Assets/Shareholders' equity (times) – 'Assets to Equity Ratio'	2.75	3.40	3.41	3.20
1 × 2 × 3 = ROE (%)	9.12	–39.65	–12.57	–8.72

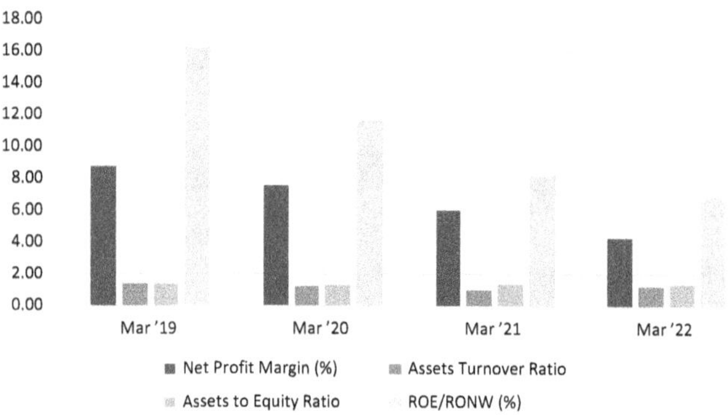

Figure 4.4 DuPont trend of MSIL

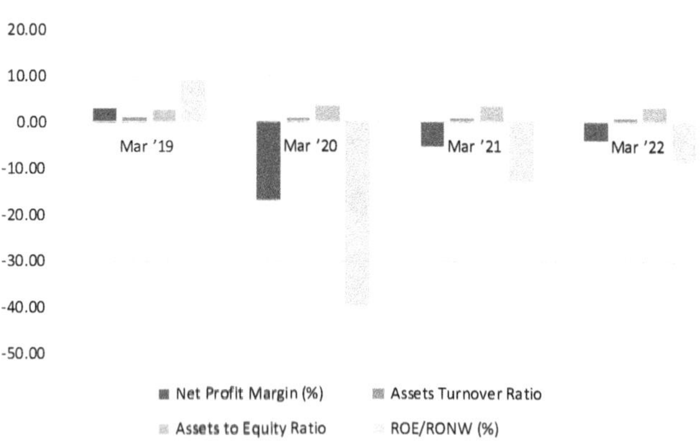

Figure 4.5 DuPont trend of TML

Analysis

- In all these years, from 2019 to 2022, MSIL generates a greater return on the funds employed as compared to TML. This can be attributed to the greater core efficiency of MSIL over the years, as discussed above.
- The positive part is that MSIL has outperformed the industry in terms of return on equity, with an exception of 2022.
- In general, a detailed insight into the efficiency of operations, demand for products and utilisation of resources is required to improve the return generation on the resources employed.

Analysis

- The return on equity for MSIL has been on the decreasing trend during these years. It indicates low performance on equity shareholders' funds.
- The decreasing ROE conveys a negative signal to the equity shareholders and affects their outlook towards the company. The declining efficiency of asset utilisation by MSIL is the main factor for the fall in ROE. From 1.37 in 2019, the 'assets turnover ratio' declined to 1.20 in 2022.
- Additionally, the nonoptimal use of financial leverage by MSIL is another main reason for the fall in ROE. The 'assets to equity ratio' remained constant at 1.36 throughout the period.
- The net profit margin has also shown a decreasing performance with other variables, contributing to the decline in ROE.

Analysis

- TML has also shown a poor performance of ROE over the years though improving in later years. With this trend, it is a much lower return-generating company for equity shareholders than MSIL.
- The asset utilisation ratio has decreased from 2019 levels of 1.14 to 0.74 in 2022. This can be attributed to factors such as a *decrease in efficiency of operations or a reduction in orders due to a slump in demand.*
- TML needs to concentrate on both, better efficiency in asset utilisation and getting more orders to improve the order-to-book ratio.

- The leverage usage is better, between 2.75 and 3.20, unlike MSIL where debt financing is at lower levels.
- The net profit margin has shown a negative trend over the years. This is way below the average of MSIL. Thus, in terms of net profitability, TML is unsound.
- The *COVID problem is common in both cases of MSIL and TML.*

Operating efficiency ratios/turnover ratios

Efficiency ratios or 'turnover ratios' are computed to find out the efficiency of the management in the utilisation of resources, both long-term and short-term. It is expected that higher turnover leads to greater profits. These are also called 'turnover ratios' as they are used to determine the efficiency of sales. These ratios are explained below.

1. INVENTORY TURNOVER RATIO (ITR)
   This ratio measures the velocity of conversion of inventory (stock) into generating sales over a period.
   It is an indication of how efficiently the inventory is managed by the company.
   It is calculated as:

ITR = Sales or Cost of goods sold*/Average inventory**

   The higher the ratio, the better it is, as it shows the efficient utilisation of inventory by the firm. When examining this ratio, it should be borne in mind that different companies will have varying levels of stock turnover depending on the industry they operate in. Low figures are generally poor as they indicate excessively high or low moving stocks.
2. AVERAGE HOLDING PERIOD (AHP)
   It indicates the number of days the company holds its inventory.
   It is calculated as:

AHP = Days in a year/ITR

A lower holding period is desirable as it leads to less obsolescence and deterioration of inventory. Days in a year are generally taken as 365 days.

[*The above two ratios are inversely related. Higher ITR will lead to lower AHP.*]

3. DEBTORS TURNOVER RATIO (DTR)/RECEIVABLES TURNOVER RATIO

This ratio indicates how quickly the firm is able to sell its products and collect its debts.

It is calculated as:

DTR = Sales/Average debtors (Average receivables)

The higher the value, the faster a company is in collecting money from debtors.

---

* COGS = Opening stock + Purchases + Direct expenses – Closing stock

** Average inventory = (Opening stock + Closing stock)/2

This is the formula for calculating the average of all ratios further.

4. AVERAGE COLLECTION PERIOD (ACP)

This ratio indicates the number of days taken by the firm in collecting its receivables.

It is calculated as:

ACP = Days in a year/DTR

A shorter collection period is preferable, because it shows higher liquidity. In general terms, the figure indicates the effectiveness of the company's credit process in collecting the money outstanding.

[*The above two ratios are inversely related. Higher DTR will lead to lower ACP.*]

5. CREDITORS TURNOVER RATIO (CTR)/PAYABLES TURNOVER RATIO

This ratio is used to measure a company's ability to get trade credit and the speed at which it pays off its suppliers.

It is calculated as:

CTR = Purchases/Average creditors (Average payables)

A lower CTR is desirable from a company's perspective because it indicates the higher credibility of the firm in the market.

6. AVERAGE PAYMENT PERIOD (APP)
This ratio indicates the average number of days in which the company makes payments to its suppliers.
It is calculated as:

APP = Days in a year/CTR

A longer payment period allows the firm to rotate the credit from the suppliers into the business. It is considered efficient.
[*The above two ratios are inversely related. Lower CTR will lead to higher APP.*]

7. WORKING CAPITAL TURNOVER RATIO (WCTR)
This ratio is used to measure the company's ability to utilise its working capital efficiently to generate revenue.
It is calculated as:

WCTR = Sales/Working capital*

* Working capital is calculated as 'current assets – current liabilities'.
The higher the ratio, the better it is, since it implies that the company is using its current resources to the fullest.

8. ASSETS TURNOVER RATIO (ATR)
The asset turnover indicates how effectively a company utilises its investment in total assets. It is a measure of how efficient the company has been in generating sales from the assets at its disposal.
It is calculated as:

ATR = Sales/Total assets

The higher the ratio, the better it is, since it implies the company is generating more revenue of its assets. A low figure would suggest either poor trading performance (which can be evaluated by the profit margin and/or sales per employee figures) or over-investment in costly fixed assets.

Efficiency ratios: *All efficiency ratios, including inventory turnover, debtors' turnover, creditors' turnover and assets turnover ratio are expressed in 'number of times'. Average holding period/collection period/payment period are denoted in 'number of days'.*

Operating efficiency analysis of Maruti Suzuki and Tata Motors

The efficiency analysis on the above parameters of the companies under study is given in Tables 4.11 and 4.12. **The financials of balance sheets and statements of profit and loss of companies, which are used and computed for the said analysis, are given in Tables 4.3–4.6.**

Table 4.11 Inventory utilisation

	Mar' 19	*Mar' 20*	*Mar' 21*	*Mar' 22*
(i) Inventory Turnover Ratio (in times)				
MSIL	18.12	16.25	16.22	20.06
TML	10.86	7.67	8.45	8.78
Industry	14.47	12.04	11.84	13.91
(ii) Average Inventory Holding Period (in days)				
MSIL	20	22	22	18
TML	34	48	43	42
Industry	25	30	31	26

Notes:

1. Automobile industry figures are taken from the 'Capitaline' *(https://awsone.capitaline.com)* database.
2. Since, COGS = Opening stock + Purchases + Direct expenses – Closing stock. Therefore, COGS above is calculated as the sum total of the cost of materials consumed + purchase of products for sale + changes in inventories.

Table 4.12 Debtors' management

	Mar' 19	*Mar' 20*	*Mar' 21*	*Mar' 22*
(i) **Debtors Turnover Ratio** (in times)				
MSIL	37.23	33.81	41.33	53.40
TML	21.29	16.80	23.13	22.51
Industry	20.88	20.09	22.76	26.03
(ii) **Average Collection Period** (in days)				
MSIL	10	11	9	7
TML	17	22	16	16
Industry	17	18	16	14

Note: Automobile industry figures are taken from the 'Capitaline' *(https://awsone.capitaline.com)* database.

Analysis

- In terms of inventory turnover efficiency, MSIL beats TML and the industry hands down. TML scores low on both fronts.
- TML needs to improve its efficiency in utilising its stock resources to gain maximum productivity out of them. It needs to look into its inventory management system and restructure the purchase and utilisation system of inventory. Its inventory holding period is much higher than the MSIL average. This increases the cost of storage and leads to losses due to obsolescence.
- MSIL not only has an average holding period of 21 days, which is lower than industry average, but it also has a sufficient margin period to purchase inventory in a scenario of sudden shortage and even least affected by COVID.

Analysis

- The average collection period of TML does not stand comparable to MSIL. That is reflected in MSIL having an average collection of merely 9 days due to a higher debtors' turnover ratio.
- TML, on the other hand, is a part of a much larger group, which allows its customers leeway to make payments. Its average collection period is higher than the industry average. It should aggressively work towards faster realisation of payments from customers.
- Thus, as far as collection is concerned, MSIL is ahead of TML. This effect is largely supported by its efficient use of resources.

Liquidity ratios

These ratios are oriented towards evaluating the short-term sustainability of the company. They provide information about a firm's ability to meet its short-term financial obligations. They are of immense use to those extending short-term credit to the firm. These ratios are as follows.

1. CURRENT RATIO
   It is calculated as:

Current assets/Current liabilities

   It reflects the working capital situation and indicates the ability of a company to pay its short-term creditors from the realisation of its current assets. *An ideal figure is 2:1,* which indicates that there are sufficient assets available to pay liabilities.

   Current assets primarily include inventory, trade receivables and cash and bank balances.

   Current liabilities mainly include short-term debts, account payables and so forth.

   In the 'retail and manufacturing sectors', the expected figures are between 1 and 1.6; in the 'wholesale and construction sectors', it is between 1.1 and 1.5; and in the 'automobile sector', it is around 1.2. Generally, where credit terms and large stocks are common to the business, the current ratio will be higher than, *for example*, a trading business where credit sales are the norm.
2. LIQUID RATIO/ACID-TEST RATIO/QUICK RATIO
   It is calculated as:

Liquid Assets (*Current Assets – Stock – Prepaid Expenses*)/ Current Liabilities

   It is generally considered to be a more accurate assessment of a company's financial health than the current ratio *as it excludes relatively low liquid items like stock (inventory) and prepaid expenses,* thus reducing the risk of relying on a ratio that may include slow-moving or redundant stock items.

An ideal ratio is 1. In the 'manufacturing sector', figures between 0.7 and 1.1 are seen as acceptable, and for the 'wholesale sector' it is between 0.7 and 1.0. The 'construction sector' operates between 0.6 and 1.0.

3. SUPER-QUICK RATIO/CASH RATIO
   It is calculated as:

Cash and Bank/Current Liabilities

   It is the closest indicator of liquidity of a firm as it focuses only on 'cash and bank balances' availability to meet current liabilities. The IT/ITES sector has the highest cash ratio among all the sectors.

Liquidity ratios: *All liquidity ratios are expressed in number of times.*

Liquidity analysis of Maruti Suzuki and Tata Motors

The liquidity analysis on the above parameters of the companies under study is given in Table 4.13. **The financials used and computed for the said analysis, are given earlier in Tables 4.3–4.6.**

Table 4.13 Liquidity analysis

	Mar' 19	*Mar' 20*	*Mar' 21*	*Mar' 22*
(i) Current Ratio (in times)				
MSIL	0.87	0.75	1.15	0.99
TML	0.58	0.53	0.60	0.58
Industry	1.46	1.52	1.48	1.42
(ii) Liquid Ratio (in times)				
MSIL	0.64	0.46	0.96	0.78
TML	0.37	0.38	0.43	0.44
Industry	0.84	0.89	0.91	0.91

Note: Automobile industry figures are taken from the 'Capitaline' *(https://awsone.capitaline.com)* and 'Ace Analyser' *(https://www.aceanalyser.com)* databases.

Analysis

- MSIL shows better liquidity than TML. But both the companies have lower liquidity ratios than the industry average.
- Both MSIL and TML have 20–30% lower quick ratios than current ratios, indicating a reasonable quantum of receivables.

Solvency ratios

These ratios are used to find out the long-term soundness of a company. They measure how financially sound a company is to meet its long-term obligations and are also known as 'leverage ratios'. They include *debt ratios*, which are based on the 'balance sheet', and *coverage ratios*, which are based on the 'income statement'.

A high degree of solvency indicates that a company's cash flows are consistent enough to pay periodic interest and principal repayments on its debt. These ratios are very significant to banks and financial institutions for lending activity.

These ratios are discussed as follows.

1. DEBT-EQUITY RATIO (D/E RATIO)
   It is calculated as:

Long-term Debt/Equity (Net Worth)

   The D/E ratio indicates the relative proportions of debt and equity in financing the assets of a firm and the extent to which the firm depends upon debt capital for its existence. In other words, it reveals whether the firm is 'highly leveraged' or not, that is the benefit of *trading on equity* is there or not. It also indicates the margin of safety to the creditors, that is the extent to which the creditors face risk in getting their due money back.

This is a measurement of a company's equity-liability relationship and is helpful to investors looking for a quick take on a company's leverage. A high debt/equity ratio generally means that a company has been aggressive in financing its growth with debt. The higher the ratio, the greater will be the risk to the creditors, and this indicates too much dependence of the firm on debt capital. *The accepted ratio is taken as 2:1.*

The debt-to-equity ratio also depends on the industry in which the company operates. *For example*, 'airlines and power sector companies' tend to have a debt/equity ratio above 2:1, while 'software companies' have a negligible debt-to-equity ratio.

2. INTEREST COVERAGE RATIO (ICR)

The interest coverage ratio gives an idea about a company's ability to pay interest on its overdue debt.

It is computed as:

EBIT/Interest on long-term loans

The greater the ratio, the greater the safety of the lender's interest, as it shows the borrower's ability to pay its debt expenses. On the other hand, a lower ratio shows the company is in poor light, as it is going to struggle to pay its debt expenses.

3. DEBT SERVICE COVERAGE RATIO (DSCR)

It is the amount of cash flow available to meet annual interest and principal repayments on debt, including sinking fund payments. *This ratio should ideally be over 1.* That would mean there is enough income to pay the debt obligations.

DSCR is calculated as:

Cash Flow from Operating activities after TAX/ (Interest Payments + Instalments)

The DSCR is an extension of the interest coverage ratio, *but it is a better ratio for solvency than ICR*. It is commonly used by banks and financial institutions for loan purposes.

DSCR mechanism

In calculating *DSCR*:

'Interest' refers to interest on long-term loans. It is easily available in the statement of profit and loss.

'Instalments' include the principal repayments and lease repayments of the borrowings that are due upon the company. Instalments cannot be accurately determined from the balance sheet of the firm or from the income statement, as principal and lease repayments are not reflected in the income statement. The instalment figure is available in the *Cash Flow (from financing activities) Statement of the firm*, in which they are shown under the head 'Repayment of Long-Term Borrowings'.

Significance of DSCR:

- DSCR is used by banks and financial institutions giving long-term finance to organisations.
- This ratio is calculated to gauge the capability of the organisation to repay the dues arising as a result of long-term borrowings.
- A high debt service ratio assures the lenders a regular and periodical interest income.

On the other hand, a low DSCR indicates the insufficient earning capacity of the organisations to meet the obligations of long-term borrowings.

Solvency ratios: *All solvency ratios are expressed in number of times.*

Solvency analysis of Maruti Suzuki and Tata Motors

The analysis of solvency of the companies under study is given in Table 4.14. **The financials of balance sheets and statements of profit and loss of companies, which are used and computed for the said analysis, are given earlier in Tables 4.3–4.6.**

Analysis

- MSIL has a much lower D/E ratio than both TML and the industry average. MSIL is almost a zero-debt company. Further, it has been decreasing over the years, indicating greater reliance on internal financing than debt.
- Both in terms of covering its interests and capital borrowed, MSIL beats both TML and the industry again by a large margin. This is due to its higher interest coverage ratio. In fact, TML shows a negative ICR due to negative operating profit in later years. Thus, for a lending institution, MSIL would be a safe bet.

Market performance ratios

Every company strives to maximise the shareholders' value. *Shareholders' value* is directly linked to the market performance of a company, particularly in publicly held companies.

Table 4.14 Solvency analysis

	Mar' 19	*Mar' 20*	*Mar' 21*	*Mar' 22*
(i) **D/E Ratio** (in times)				
MSIL	0.06	0.06	0.05	0.04
TML	0.71	1.00	1.04	0.85
Industry	0.31	0.30	0.33	0.30
(ii) **Interest Coverage Ratio** (in times)				
MSIL	105.28	23.90	22.95	23.15
TML	0.54	-2.51	-1.27	-0.49
Industry	12.69	6.50	5.70	10.06

Note: Automobile industry figures are taken from the 'Capitaline' *(https://awsone.capitaline.com)* database.

Market ratios are used to determine the market performance (valuation) of a company in the securities market. They indicate the market standing of the company for shareholders' wealth. These are as follows:

1. BOOK VALUE PER SHARE (BV)
   It measures the net worth to be enjoyed by the ordinary shareholders of the company after all its debts are paid. In simple terms, it would be the amount of money that a holder of an equity share would get in case of liquidation of the company.
   It is defined as:

Book value per share = Net Worth/Number of Equity shares

2. PRICE TO BOOK RATIO (P/B)
   It is a valuation ratio expressed as a multiple (i.e., how many times a company's stock is trading per share as compared to the company's book value per share).
   It is computed as:

Price to Book value = Market price per equity share/ Book value per equity share

   It is used by the investors to find out what they are paying for each share compared to the real value of the firm.
3. PRICE TO EARNINGS RATIO (P/E)
   The price to earnings ratio, often called the P/E ratio or P/E multiple, is a market prospect ratio that calculates the market value of a stock relative to its earnings. It shows what the market is willing to pay for a stock based on its current earnings. This ratio is widely used in the valuation of a company for current investments. It is defined as:

Price to Earnings = Market price per equity share/ Earnings per equity share

   The investors often use this ratio to evaluate what a stock's fair market value should be by predicting future earnings per share. It determines the under-valuation or over-valuation of a company.

4. DIVIDEND YIELD RATIO (D/Y)

Dividend yield ratio (D/Y ratio) refers to the amount of dividend paid per share with respect to the market price per share. It denotes how much cash flow you are getting for each rupee invested in an equity share. It is calculated as:

Dividend Yield Ratio (D/Y Ratio) = DPS /MPS

Market ratios: *BV per share is expressed as Rs. per share.*

P/B and P/E are expressed in number of times as they are multiples.

D/Y is expressed in percentage.

Market analysis of Maruti Suzuki and Tata Motors

The securities market performance of the companies under study is analysed in Tables 4.15–4.17. **The financials of balance sheets and statements of profit and loss of companies, which are used and computed for the said analysis, are given earlier in Tables 4.3–4.6.**

Table 4.15 Closing 'market price' as of March of the AY (Rs. per share) (BSE)

	Mar' 13	*Mar' 14*	*Mar' 15*	*Mar' 16*
MSIL	6,671.70	4,287.75	6,859.75	7,559.90
TML	174.30	71.05	301.85	433.50

Table 4.16 Price/earnings ratio (in times)

	Mar' 19	*Mar' 20*	*Mar' 21*	*Mar' 22*
MSIL	26.87	22.92	48.99	60.63
TML	29.34	-3.37	-45.80	-119.42

Table 4.17 Price/book value (in times)

	Mar' 19	*Mar' 20*	*Mar' 21*	*Mar' 2*
MSIL	4.37	2.67	4.03	4.22
TML	2.67	1.46	6.07	8.34

Note: P/B figures are taken from the 'Ace Analyser' *(https://www.aceanalyser.com)* database.

Analysis

- The 'price to earnings' ratio is positive and very high, almost crossing 50 times in 2022 in the case of MSIL as compared to TML throughout the time period. The valuation of MSIL seems to be very high due to a dip in the earnings. For TML, the ratio has gone negative during the last three years due to a continuous decline in earnings per share. Though it is not a good sign, even the best companies go through periods when they are unprofitable. That does not mean that they have become a bad investment, and this is reflected in the increasing market price of TML. Thus, the company is a promising longer-term prospect.
- The price-to-book value tells another story. MSIL seems to be underpriced as compared to TML. But the EPS of TML is reducing from – Rs. 21.06 in 2020 to – Rs. 3.63 in 2022, and its increasing market value shows that it is a better proposition as investors from a long-term perspective look at growth. Also, for short-term investors, the volatility is a deterrent.

'Golden Rules' of financial analysis

- **Analyse a company in totality, not in segments.**
- **Compare a firm's performance with that of its peers, that is compare ratios in the industry.**
- **Study the trend of ratios for analysing the growth pattern of the firm.**
- **Evaluate ratios with benchmarks, if any.**

- Analyse the reasons for the performance of ratios.
- Focus on deviations in ratios.
- Correlate the numbers with business performance.
- Look at the management of the company for strengths, weaknesses, opportunities, and threats (SWOT) and FUTURE OUTLOOK.

Financial forecasting

Financial forecasting is the process adopted by firms for planning their future financial activities. The forecasting process provides the means for a firm to express its goals to be achieved next year or in the long term and to ensure that they are internally consistent. It also assists the firm in identifying the asset requirements and needs for external financing.

Sales forecast – 'Percentage of Sales method'

The principal driver of the forecasting process is generally the 'sales forecast'. Therefore, the common forecasting approach used by the firms is the 'Percentage of Sales method'. It forecasts the Balance Sheet and Income Statement by assuming that most accounts maintain a fixed proportion of Sales.

$$\boxed{\text{Forecasted Sales S1} = \text{S0}\ (1 + g)}$$

(i) Since Balance Sheets and Income Statements are largely related to sales, the forecasting process can help the firm in assessing the requirement of 'Current and Fixed Assets' needed to support the forecasted sales level.

(ii) Accordingly, the decision about 'Capital Structure', that is how much external financing will be needed, in addition to or above the internal financing, to pay for the forecasted increase in assets, can be determined.

CASE LET

E Ltd., an Indian conglomerate, has finalised its results for the year 2014–15. As yearly practice, their finance department is geared up for financial forecasting of the results for 2015–16 in order to plan out their actions better for achieving next year's goals. They have used the 'Percentage of Sales' approach, assuming a 19% growth rate in sales based on net profit margin.

The Statement of Profit and Loss and Balance Sheet of E Ltd. for the year 2014–15 are given in Figures 4.6 and 4.7.

Solution:

The 'forecasted financial statements' for the year 2016, based on the financial statements of 2015, are given in Figures 4.8 and 4.9.

Statement of Profit and Loss of E Ltd. for the year ended 2015

(Rs. In million)

Particulars	2014–15
REVENUE	
Turnover	2,500
TOTAL REVENUE	2,500
EXPENSES	
Costs	1,900
TOTAL EXPENSES	1,900
Profit before tax	600
Tax	143
Profit after tax (PAT)	457
Dividends	321
Retained Earnings	136
Other Information:	
Forecasted Growth Rate in Sales: 19%	

Figure 4.6 Statement of profit and loss of E Ltd. for 2015

Balance Sheet of E Ltd. as at 31st March, 2015

(Rs. in million)

Particulars	2015
ASSETS	
Non-Current Assets	
Fixed Assets	
(i) Tangible Assets, Net	1,800
Current Assets	
Inventories	900
Trade Receivables	500
Cash and Bank Balances	500
	1,900
TOTAL	3,700
EQUITY AND LIABILITIES	
Shareholders' Funds	
Share Capital	650
Reserves and Surplus	800
	1,450
Non-Current Liabilities	
Long-Term Borrowings	580
Current Liabilities	
Short-Term Borrowings	1,170
Trade Payables	500
	1,670
TOTAL	3,700
Other Information:	
External Financing Needed	446

Figure 4.7 Balance sheet of E Ltd. as of 2015

'Forecasted' Statement of Profit and Loss of E Ltd.

(Rs. in million)

Particulars	2014–15	2015–16
REVENUE		
Turnover	2,500	2,975
TOTAL REVENUE	2,500	2,975
EXPENSES		
Costs	1,900	2,261
TOTAL EXPENSES	1,900	2,261
Profit before tax	600	714
Tax	143	170
Profit after tax (PAT)	457	544
Dividends	321	382
Retained Earnings	136	162

Figure 4.8 Forecasted statement of profit and loss of E Ltd. for 2016

Note: For financial forecasting, as mentioned above, the 'Percentage of Sales' approach is used, assuming a 19% growth rate in sales based on net profit margin.

'Forecasted' Balance Sheet of E Ltd.

(Rs. in million)

Particulars	2015	2016
ASSETS		
Non-Current Assets		
Fixed Assets		
(i) Tangible Assets, Net	1,800	2,142
Current Assets		
Inventories	900	1,071
Trade Receivables	500	595

Figure 4.9 Forecasted balance sheet of E Ltd. for 2016

'Forecasted' Balance Sheet of E Ltd.

(Rs. in million)

Particulars	2015	2016
Cash and Bank Balances	500	595
	1,900	2,261
TOTAL	3,700	4,403
EQUITY AND LIABILITIES		
Shareholders' Funds		
Share Capital	650	650
Reserves and Surplus	800	962
	1,450	1,612
Non-Current Liabilities		
Long-Term Borrowings	580	580
Current Liabilities		
Short-Term Borrowings	1,170	1,170
Trade Payables	500	595
	1,670	1,765
TOTAL	3,700	3,957

Figure 4.9 (Continued)

Revised balance sheet for 2016: It is clear in the above forecasted balance sheet for the year 2016 that there is a shortage of expected funds of Rs. 446 million* to finance the asset requirements for the next year. The company has to decide now whether it will finance it from short-term or long-term financing.

Being short-term funds to be repaid at current intervals, E Ltd. decides to finance it from long-term external borrowing. This will increase its present long-term borrowings from Rs. 580 million to Rs. 1,026 million. This will provide E Ltd. the necessary funds to finance their assets for next year's sales and growth.

*(Total assets = Rs. 4403 – Total funds = 3957)

The 'revised' forecasted balance sheet for the year 2016, after incorporating the funds requirements for the assets as discussed above, is given in Figure 4.10.

'Forecasted' Balance Sheet of E Ltd. (Revised)

(Rs. in million)

Particulars	2015	2016
ASSETS		
Non-Current Assets		
Fixed Assets		
(i) Tangible Assets, Net	1,800	2,142
Current Assets		
Inventories	900	1,071
Trade Receivables	500	595
Cash and Bank Balances	500	595
	1,900	2,261
TOTAL	3,700	4,403
EQUITY AND LIABILITIES		
Shareholders' Funds		
Share Capital	650	650
Reserves and Surplus	800	962
	1,450	1,612
Non-Current Liabilities		
Long-Term Borrowings	580	1,026
Current Liabilities		
Short-Term Borrowings	1,170	1,170
Trade Payables	500	595
	1,670	1,765
TOTAL	3,700	4,403

Figure 4.10 Revised forecasted balance sheet of E Ltd. for 2016

Corporate cases

This section discusses cases from corporate India for further learning into the subject.

It analyses the financial performance of select companies in the 'Indian service sector' on a comparative basis. Their financial issues and challenges will be different from the manufacturing sector companies, like Maruti Suzuki and Tata Motors, as discussed above. Two sectors have been taken here: telecom and banking. **The financials of the companies have been taken from the** 'Capitaline' *(https://awsone.capitaline.com)* and 'Ace Analyser' **(https://www.aceanalyser.com) databases.**

The companies analysed here are multinational corporations (MNCs), so their analysis is relevant to the international users

Indian telecom sector

The telecommunication industry of India is the world's fastest-growing telecom industry. In the Indian telecom sector, the financial analysis of Bharti Airtel Ltd. and Vodafone Idea Ltd. has been done on a comparative basis. Bharti Airtel is the largest cellular provider in India and the world's third-largest, single-country mobile operator. Vodafone Idea is a leading GSM (Global System for Mobile Communications) company in India. The company was created on 31st August, 2018, by the merger of Vodafone India and Idea Cellular of Aditya Birla Group, to form a new entity called Vodafone Idea Ltd.

Profitability

The profitability of these companies is being discussed with the help of various sales-based and assets-based profitability ratios as

Table 4.18 EBITDA ratio of Airtel and Vodafone Idea (%)

	Mar 19	*Mar 20*	*Mar 21*	*Mar 22*
Airtel	41.38	41.20	47.22	49.72
Vodafone Idea	11.72	34.47	39.95	40.80

Table 4.19 EBIT ratio of Airtel and Vodafone Idea (%)

	Mar 19	*Mar 20*	*Mar 21*	*Mar 22*
Airtel	10.90	3.65	13.02	15.35
Vodafone Idea	-27.37	-18.95	-15.02	-19.00

Table 4.20 Net profit ratio of Airtel and Vodafone Idea (%)

	Mar 19	*Mar 20*	*Mar 21*	*Mar 22*
Airtel	1.89	10.04	-24.47	-2.77
Vodafone Idea	-43.42	-92.56	-58.14	-73.88

Table 4.21 ROI/ROCE of Airtel and Vodafone Idea (%)

	Mar 19	*Mar 20*	*Mar 21*	*Mar 22*
Airtel	3.01	0.96	3.79	5.09
Vodafone Idea	0.00	0.00	0.00	0.00

Table 4.22 ROE of Airtel and Vodafone Idea (%)

	Mar 19	*Mar 20*	*Mar 21*	*Mar 22*
Airtel	0.93	5.46	-17.61	-2.58
Vodafone Idea	0.00	0.00	0.00	0.00

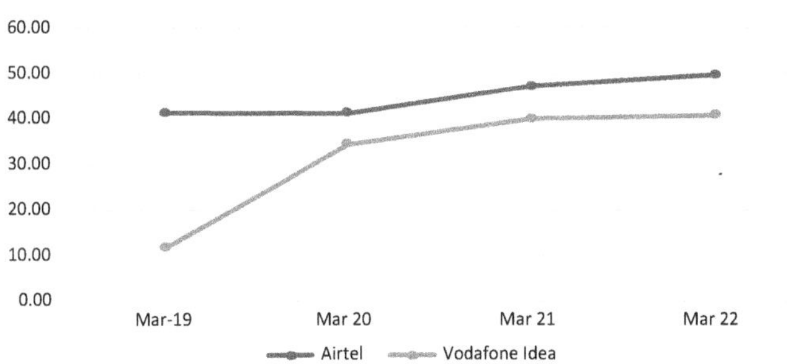

Figure 4.11 EBITDA trend of Airtel and Vodafone Idea

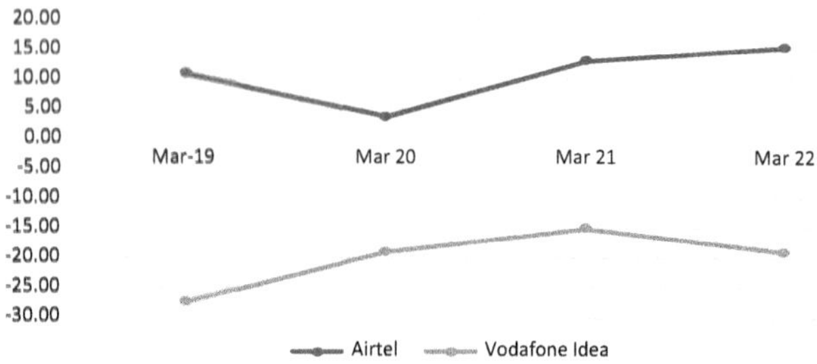

Figure 4.12 EBIT trend of Airtel and Vodafone Idea

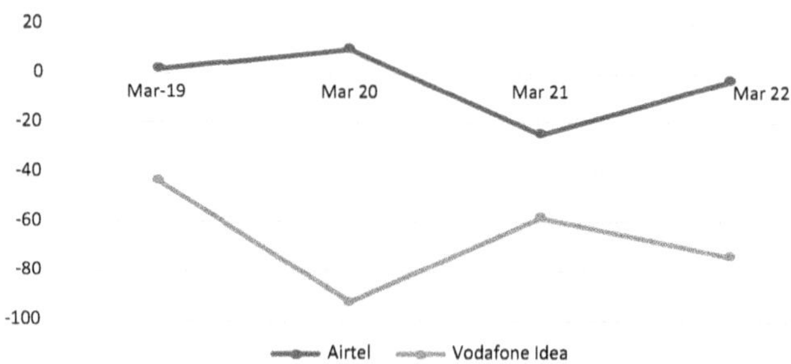

Figure 4.13 Net profit trend of Airtel and Vodafone Idea

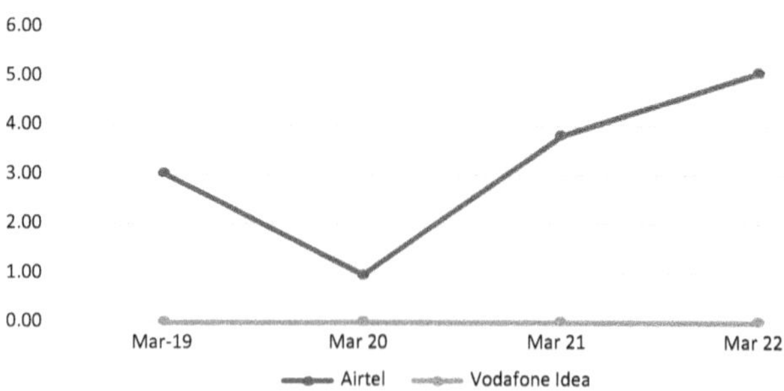

Figure 4.14 ROI trend of Airtel and Vodafone Idea

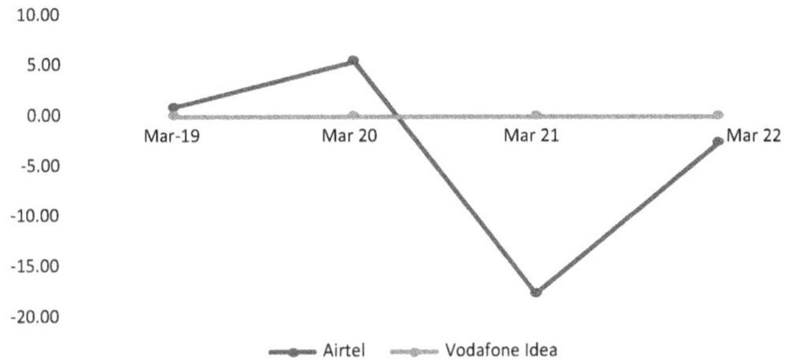

Figure 4.15 ROE trend of Airtel and Vodafone Idea

given in the following Tables 4.18–4.22. Their trends are given in Figures 4.11–4.15.

EBITDA RATIO

EBITDA margin for Airtel is higher than that of Vodafone Idea's, indicating a better operating profit cushion to meet expenses, though the margins of both the companies have shown an increasing trend during the period under study.

EBIT RATIO

Airtel is better placed with regard to EBIT margin as well. It is not only positive but shows an increasing performance with an exception of 2020. The alarming part for Vodafone Idea is that its margin has been negative throughout the span of four years as compared to Airtel, though it has declined.

NET PROFIT RATIO

Here also, Airtel is better placed than Vodafone Idea regarding the net profit ratio. It is a good sign for stakeholders, including the company itself, for future growth. But there is also a worrying sign for Airtel: its net profit margin has reduced lately and turned negative in the last two years of 2021 and 2022. Vodafone Ide has much greater negative profit margins during the period under study.

ROI RATIO/ROCE RATIO

ROI/ROCE is better for Airtel than Vodafone Idea. It shows better utilisation of resources and higher return on capital employed by the management as evident in profit margins above. Due to negative EBIT, the ratio is zero for Vodafone Idea.

RETURN ON EQUITY RATIO

Once again, Airtel has shown more promise for shareholders' interest in the company in the years of 2019 and 2020, but then it goes negative. The negative PAT leads to this ratio as zero for Vodafone Idea.

Conclusion

Bharti Airtel's outlook is promising in line with the future growth potential of the sector. Its profitability at various levels has been better than Vodafone Idea's. The business models of telecom operators as a whole are being stress-tested by overcapacity-led hyper-competition. With several licensees operating at tariffs lower than cost, the eventual phasing out of this period of over-capacity is inevitable.

Indian banking sector

The banking system remains the most dominant segment of the financial sector worldwide. Indian banks continue to build on their strengths under the regulator's watchful eye and, hence, have emerged stronger. *The Indian banking sector, in addition to being governed by the Companies Act, 1956 and 2013, is also governed by the Banking Regulation Act, 1949. Their financial statements and indicators are different from a non-banking sector company. This makes the financial analysis of their performance more challenging.*

The present study analyses the financial performance of *State Bank of India (SBI)* and *ICICI Bank* on a comparative basis, the former being in the public sector and the latter being in the private sector. SBI is the largest state-owned banking company in India. ICICI Bank is a leading bank in the private sector.

Profitability

Profitability of the banks under study has been discussed with the help of the following ratios, as given in Tables 4.23 and 4.24.

ROE

ROE for both the banks has shown an increasing trend during the period. But the higher ROE of ICICI Bank indicates better returns to the shareholders.

EPS

SBI's EPS in the years 2020 and 2022 has been greater than that of ICICI Bank's. In all the years, for both SBI and ICICI Bank, the EPS has been moving upwards despite the COVID period.

Table 4.23 Profitability ratios of SBI

	Mar 19	*Mar 20*	*Mar 21*	*Mar 22*
1. ROE (%)	0.35	6.74	9.02	12.91
2. EPS (Rs.)	0.97	16.23	22.87	35.49
3. DPS (Rs.)	0.00	0.00	4.00	7.10

Table 4.24 Profitability ratios of ICICI Bank

	Mar 19	*Mar 20*	*Mar 21*	*Mar 22*
1. ROE (%)	3.24	7.25	12.56	14.97
2. EPS (Rs.)	5.22	12.25	23.41	33.59
3. DPS (Rs.)	1.00	0.00	2.00	5.00

DPS

Like EPS, the same trend can be observed in DPS of both the banks. But the dividend payment of SBI is better than that of ICICI Bank in the current two years, hence a larger share of the earnings of SBI is distributed as dividends to its shareholders as compared to that of ICICI Bank. This is generally seen as a good trend for investors with a preference for current income.

Banking performance

As mentioned earlier, *the banking sector company's financial statements and indicators are different from a non-banking sector company*. So, in addition to the profitability ratios discussed above, 'core banking ratios' of the units under study are discussed in Tables 4.25 and 4.26. These ratios are relevant for analysing the performance of banking companies.

INTEREST EXPENDED/INTEREST EARNED

This ratio indicates the potential of earnings of the banks by way of interest paid or received from the deposits and loans of the bank. A lower ratio of interest expended/interest earned indicates higher efficiency of the bank in managing and matching interest expenditure and interest income. The reducing trend of both the banks is visible during the time span. But SBI indicates higher efficiency in managing the interest expenditure and

Table 4.25 Banking ratios of SBI

	Mar 19	*Mar 20*	*Mar 21*	*Mar 22*
1. Interest Expended/Interest Earned (%)	63.62	61.88	58.25	56.18
2. Credit to Deposit Ratio (%)	73.35	73.32	68.97	67.03
3. CAR (Capital Adequacy Ratio) (%)	12.72	13.06	13.74	13.83
4. Net NPA Ratio (Net Non-Performing Assets/Net Advances) (%)	3.01	2.23	1.50	1.02

Table 4.26 Banking ratios of ICICI Bank

	Mar 19	*Mar 20*	*Mar 21*	*Mar 22*
1. Interest Expended/Interest Earned (%)	57.39	55.52	50.72	45.05
2. Credit to Deposit Ratio (%)	90.54	86.52	80.95	79.75
3. CAR (Capital Adequacy Ratio) (%)	16.89	16.11	19.12	19.16
4. Net NPA Ratio (Net Non-Performing Assets/Net Advances) (%)	2.29	1.54	1.24	0.81

earnings. This would have a strong effect on the bottom line of the company.

CREDIT TO DEPOSIT RATIO

The ratio is indicative of the percentage of funds lent by the bank out of the total amount raised through deposits. A higher ratio reflects the ability of the bank to make optimal use of the available resources and hence the possibility of earning higher returns through its resources. Here, it can be seen that a higher and increasing percentage of the amount received through deposits is utilised by ICICI Bank as compared to SBI.

CAPITAL ADEQUACY RATIO (CAR)

This is the capital to risk weighted assets ratio, which signifies the risk exposure of the bank. Its minimum limit prescribed by the RBI is 9% for scheduled banks. The higher the ratio, the greater the capacity of the bank to absorb losses. As can be seen, the CAR of ICICI Bank is higher than that of SBI. A bank's capital is the cushion it provides for potential losses to its depositors. Being a private company, it's a good sign for ICICI Bank to have a higher CAR

From 2019 onwards, both banks have shown an increase in CAR probably on account of two factors: *(i) the Indian banking sector is in the restructuring phase on account of bad loans and (ii) they will need additional capital to comply with the Basel-III norms.*

NET NPA RATIO

The net non-performing assets to loans (advances) ratio is used as a measure of the overall quality of the bank's loan book. Net NPAs are calculated by reducing the cumulative balance of provisions outstanding at a period end from gross NPAs. A higher ratio reflects a rising bad quality of loans. Thus, in the long run, the bank has high chances of huge losses. ICICI Bank scores better than SBI, and it can be inferred that the loans issued by ICICI Bank are quality loans, and there is a higher probability of earning returns from those loans.

Conclusion

SBI shows higher efficiency over ICICI Bank in managing interest expenditure with improvement in earnings, but ICICI Bank scores in areas of deposits' utilisation, capital cushion and loan management. The public sector banks (PSBs), which are the base of the banking sector in India, account for a major share of the total banking industry assets. Therefore, they have to really look at cleaning the excessive non-performing assets (NPAs), with private sector banks for future stability of the banking sector in India.

References

1 IBEF. 2023. *Automobile Industry in India*. https://www.ibef.org/industry/india-automobiles (accessed on 26 July 2023).

Glossary

Accounting It is the art of recording, classifying and summarising in a significant manner and in terms of money, transactions and events, which are, in part, at least of a financial character and interpreting the results thereof.

Accounting Principles There are basic accounting principles and guidelines that govern the field of accounting. These are referred to as 'generally accepted accounting principles' (GAAP).

Accrual Basis of Accounting Under this basis, income is recorded when a sale is made, irrespective of the receipt, and expenses are recorded when they are incurred, without being paid.

Amortisation It is used for writing off and replacing intangible assets.

Assets They are resources that are owned by a business, have a commercial value and are used for generating returns.

Assets Turnover Ratio (ATR) It is a measure of how efficient the company has been in generating sales from the assets at its disposal.

Associate Company An associate company is one whose 20% or more shares are owned by a holding company.

Authorised Share Capital It is the maximum limit that the company is registered with the Registrar of Companies to raise.

Average Collection Period (ACP) This ratio indicates the number of days taken by the firm in collecting its receivables.

Average Holding Period (AHP) It indicates the number of days the company holds its inventory.

Average Payment Period (APP) This ratio indicates the average number of days in which the company makes payments to its suppliers.

Balance Sheet (or position statement) It depicts the economic resources owned by an entity and the claims against those resources, that is liabilities and owners' equity.

Bookkeeping It refers to the recording of business transactions only. It is a part of accounting.

Book Value per Share (BV) It measures the net worth to be enjoyed by the ordinary shareholders of the company after all debts are paid.

Bottom Line It is the net profit of the company, left for distribution to shareholders and reinvestment for future growth.

Business Organisation (also known as business enterprise, business undertaking, business firm or business concern) It is an enterprise that makes, distributes or provides any article or service, which the other members of the community need and are able and willing to pay for.

Capital It is the money contributed by owners. It is the shareholders' funds in a business.

Cash Basis of Accounting In a cash accounting method, income and expenses are recorded only when funds are received or disbursed.

CapitalWorkinProgress(CWIP) Thisincludesunder-construction or under-completion of fixed assets.

Cash Flow Statement It describes the enterprise's cash flow position during the time period.

Cash Inflows These are expected returns from the operating activities.

Cash Outflows These are outlays that result from investment activities.

Common-size Analysis (or vertical analysis) It is the analysis of financial statements on a vertical basis to determine the contribution of each item of the financial statement to total resources or with regard to a common base.

Cooperative Organisation A cooperative society is a voluntary association of persons who join hands together to carry on a commercial activity.

Cost of Goods Sold (COGS) It means the cost, to the company, of the merchandise that is sold to customers.

Credit It is the portion of a transaction that accounts for the increase in income, liabilities and equity and the decrease in assets and expenses.

Creditors Turnover Ratio (CTR) This ratio is used to measure a company's ability to get trade credit and the speed at which it pays off its suppliers.

Current Assets These are meant for current use and for day-to-day operations and are for less than a year.

Current Liability These liabilities are for less than a year.

Current Ratio It indicates the ability of a company to pay its short-term creditors from the realisation of its current assets.

Debit It is the portion of a transaction that accounts for the increase in assets and expenses and the decrease in liabilities, equity and income.

Debt-Equity Ratio (D/E) It indicates the relative proportions of debt and equity in financing the assets of a firm.

Debt Service Coverage Ratio (DCSR) It is the amount of cash flow available to meet annual interest and principal payments on 'debt'.

Debtors Turnover Ratio (DTR) This ratio indicates how quickly the firm is able to sell its products and collect its debts.

Departmental Undertaking It is a public sector enterprise that is managed by government officials under the supervision of the head of the department concerned.

Depletion It refers to the process of writing off and replacing natural resources.

Depreciation It means 'the reduction in or loss of quality or value of a fixed asset through physical wear and tear in use or passage of time or from any other cause'. It is basically used for tangible assets.

Depreciation Accounting It is the process of writing off the fixed asset during its life and providing funds for its replacement when it becomes unproductive.

Dividend It is the amount of profits distributed to the shareholders as 'return'. It could be an annual dividend and/or interim dividend.

Dividend Payout Ratio (D/P Ratio) It refers to the amount of dividend paid per share with respect to the earnings per share.

Dividend per Share (DPS) It is defined as the portion of the company's profit distributed to each common shareholder.

Dividend Yield Ratio (D/Y) It refers to the amount of dividend paid per share with respect to the market price per share.

Double Declining Balance Method of Depreciation Here, the depreciation expense is computed by multiplying the asset cost less accumulated depreciation by twice the straight-line rate expressed in a percentage.

Double-entry System of Accounting It is the system wherein every transaction is considered to have two effects and recorded in two accounts.

Dual Aspect Principle It is the underlying basis for double-entry accounting system and states that every transaction has two aspects: debit and credit.

Earnings Before Interest, Tax, Depreciation and Amortisation (EBITDA) This is the amount of profit earned from the core activities of business, excluding finance costs, tax and depreciation provisioning.

EBITDA Margin It measures the profitability of a concern after meeting other lines of expenses, including office and selling expenses but excluding the non-cash expenses of depreciation.

Earnings Before Interest and Tax (EBIT) (operating profit) This represents the operating profit earned during the normal course of operations after adjusting non-cash expenses of depreciation and amortisation.

Earnings per Share (EPS) It is defined as the portion of the company's profit allocated to each outstanding share of a common stock.

EBIT Margin (or operating profit ratio) It measures the profitability of a concern after charging the non-cash expenses of depreciation.

Efficiency Ratios (or turnover ratios) These are computed to find out the efficiency of the management in the utilisation of resources, both long-term and short-term.

Equity Shares (or ordinary shares or common shares) These are those shares that do not carry any special or preferential rights in the payment of annual dividend or repayment of capital.

Expenses These are the costs that are incurred to run and maintain a business.

Financial Accounting It is mainly concerned with the financial performance of an organisation and involves the preparation of financial statements of profit and loss account and the balance sheet.

Financial Analysis (or financial appraisal) It is the process of analysing the financial statements information and interpreting the meaning of those numbers with the help of financial tools.

Financial Forecasting It is the process adopted by firms for planning their future financial activities.

Financial Ratio It is a relationship between two financial elements that indicates information about business activities.

Financial Statements These are financial reports in a prescribed format required to be prepared by an entity to meet the information needs of various stakeholders.

Fixed Assets (or non-current assets) They are long-term resources, more than a year, and are used for the long-term growth and expansion of a business.

Goods and Services Tax (GST) An 'indirect tax' that has replaced many central and state indirect taxes levied on goods and services in India.

Government Company It is a company in which not less than 51% of the paid-up share capital is held by the central government or by one or more state governments or jointly by the central and state governments.

Gross Profit The gross profit represents the amount of direct profit associated with the actual manufacturing of goods.

Gross Profit Ratio This indicates the margin generated out of sales after meeting production expenses.

Holding Company It is the parent company that owns 20% or more shares of another company.

Indirect Expenses 'Overheads'. They could be manufacturing overheads, office overheads and/or selling overheads.

Intangible Fixed Assets These fixed assets are those that are not visible.

Interest Coverage Ratio (ICR) It is the ratio that gives an idea about a company's ability to pay interest on its overdue debt.

Inventory Turnover Ratio (ITR) This ratio measures the velocity of conversion of inventory into generating sales over a period.

Issued Share Capital It represents the amount actually offered to the public for subscription.

Joint Hindu Family Business It may be defined as a form of business organisation in which all the male members of a Hindu undivided family carry on business under the management and control of the head of the family called 'Karta'.

Joint Sector Enterprise It consists of those business undertakings wherein the ownership, management and control are shared jointly by the government, private entrepreneurs and the public.

Joint Stock Company It is an association of persons having a separate legal existence, perpetual succession and common seal and incorporated under the Companies Act, 1956.

Liability It is a debt or outstanding balance owed to another party, requiring a future cash flow for payment

Limited Liability Partnership (LLP) It is a corporate structure that combines the flexibility of a partnership on the basis of a mutually arrived agreement and the advantages of limited liability of a company.

Liquidity It is the availability of cash or near-cash funds for meeting the day-to-day expenses of the firm.
Liquid Ratio (or acid-test ratio or quick ratio) It assesses the company's short-term financial health based on more liquid assets, excluding stock.
Liquidity Ratios These ratios provide information about a firm's ability to meet its short-term financial obligations.
Long-term Liability (or non-current liability) These liabilities are for more than a year.
Market Ratios These ratios are used to determine the market performance of a company in the stock market.
Net Profit Margin (or PAT margin) It measures the net margin of profitability on sales.
Net Worth It represents the shareholders' funds in a company, as the total of share capital and reserves and surplus.
Non-operating Expenses These are related to the non-core activities of the business.
Non-operating Revenue It is the income that comes from the non-core activities of the business.
Operating Expenses These are the core expenses of the business.
Operating Ratio It analyses the profitability of the firm with regard to coverage of expenses.
Operating Revenue It refers to the core income of the business, that is 'turnover' or 'sales and services'.
One-person Company (OPC) It is a company with only one person as its member.
Paid-up Share Capital It is the actual amount paid up by shareholders on subscription.
Partnership In this form of ownership, two or more persons enter into a contract to carry on some lawful business jointly and to share its profits.
Preference Shares These shares carry certain special or preferential rights in the payment of dividend and repayment of capital as compared to equity shareholders.
Price to Book Ratio (P/B) It is a valuation ratio expressed as a multiple (i.e., how many times a company's stock is trading per share as compared to the company's book value per share).
Price to Earnings Ratio (P/E Multiple) It is a market prospect ratio that calculates the market value of a stock relative to its earnings.
Private Company It is a form of company that is prohibited from issuing shares to the public.

Private Enterprise It is owned, managed and controlled exclusively by private businessmen. There is no participation by the central or state governments in its establishment and ownership.
Profit It is the excess of income over expenses.
Profit Before taxes (EBT) This is the amount of profit earned by the business before taxes.
Profit After taxes (PAT) This is the 'bottom line' earnings of the business.
Profitability Ratios These ratios are used to analyse the profitability of a company in total and return generated for shareholders.
Public Company It is a form of company that is free to invite the general public to subscribe to its shares and debentures.
Public Enterprise It may be defined as an enterprise which may be owned by the state, managed by the state or owned and managed by the state.
Ratio Analysis It involves computing 'financial ratios' and analysing the business performance based on them.
Reserves and Surplus (or retained earnings) This represents the amount of profit undistributed to the shareholders and kept aside for future growth.
Return on Capital Employed (ROCE) It measures whether or not a company is generating adequate profits in relation to the funds invested in it.
Return on Equity (ROE) It indicates whether or not a company is generating enough return for them.
Revenue (or income) It is the money that comes in on account of sales of goods or provision of services.
Share It is one of the units into which the share capital of a company can be divided.
Share Capital The share capital of company represents the funds of a company raised through the issue of shares, either common or preference shares.
Single-entry System of Accounting It is the system wherein only one aspect of a transaction is recognised.
Sole Proprietorship In this form of a business enterprise, one person provides the entire capital, bears all the risks and manages the business.
Solvency It implies the long-term soundness of the firm, that is its ability to pay interest on long-term loans and repay these loans at regular intervals.

Solvency Ratios (or leverage ratios) These ratios are used to find out how financially sound a company is to meet its long-term obligations.

Statement of Profit and Loss (or income statement) It is a summary of an entity's revenues generated and expenses incurred during a period whose net result is either profit or loss.

Statutory Corporation (or a public corporation) It is a body set up under a special Act of Parliament or of a state legislature.

Straight-Line Method of Depreciation (SLM) (or fixed instalment method) In this method, depreciation is charged at a fixed amount throughout the life of an asset.

Subsidiary Company A company is called to be subsidiary if 50% shares are owned by a holding company.

Sum-of-the-Years-Digits Method of Depreciation Here, depreciation is calculated by adding up the number of years of the useful economic life.

Super-quick Ratio (or cash ratio) It is the closest indicator of liquidity of a firm as it focuses only on 'cash and bank balances' availability to meet current liabilities.

Tangible Fixed Assets These include physical fixed assets, which are visible.

Top Line It refers to the total income generated by the company.

Turnover It refers to the firm's sales of goods or services.

Working Capital This means the capital used to carry out the day-to-day operations of a business.

Working Capital Turnover Ratio (WCTR) This ratio is used to measure the company's ability to utilise its working capital efficiently to generate revenue.

Written-Down-Value Method of Depreciation (WDV) (or diminishing balance method or reducing balance method) In this method, depreciation is charged at a fixed rate on the reducing balance (i.e., cost less depreciation) every year.

Index

Note: Page numbers in *italics* indicate a figure and page numbers in **bold** indicate a table on the corresponding page.

For Product Safety Concerns and Information please contact our EU representative GPSR@taylorandfrancis.com
Taylor & Francis Verlag GmbH, Kaufingerstraße 24, 80331 München, Germany

www.ingramcontent.com/pod-product-compliance
Lightning Source LLC
LaVergne TN
LVHW021131300926
849160LV00010B/962

* 9 7 8 1 0 4 1 2 2 0 0 8 4 *